ALE... ...ILLE

Masters of Social Theory
Volume 4

MASTERS OF SOCIAL THEORY

Series Editor:

Jonathan H. Turner, *University of California, Riverside*

This new series of short volumes presents prominent social theorists of the nineteenth and twentieth centuries. Current theory in sociology involves analysis of these early thinkers' work, which attests to their enduring significance. However, secondary analysis of their work is often hurried in larger undergraduate texts or presented in long scholarly portraits.

Our attempt is to provide scholarly analysis and also to summarize the basic, core idea of the individual master. Our goal is to offer both a short scholarly reference work and individual texts for undergraduate and graduate students.

In this series:

HERBERT SPENCER by Jonathan H. Turner, *University of California, Riverside*

EMILE DURKHEIM by Robert Alun Jones, *University of Illinois, Urbana-Champaign*

MAX WEBER by Randall Collins, *University of California, Riverside*

ALEXIS DE TOCQUEVILLE by Whitney Pope, *Indiana University, Bloomington*

Forthcoming volumes and their authors include the following:

VILFREDO PARETO by Charles H. Powers, *Indiana University, Bloomington*

GEORGE HERBERT MEAD by John D. Baldwin, *University of California, Santa Barbara*

KARL MARX by Richard P. Appelbaum, *University of California, Santa Barbara*

ALEXIS DE TOCQUEVILLE

His Social and Political Theory

Whitney Pope

in collaboration with Lucetta Pope

Masters of Social Theory
Volume 4

Cover Photo: Culver Pictures

SAGE PUBLICATIONS
The Publishers of Professional Social Science
Beverly Hills   London   New Delhi

For information address:

SAGE Publications, Inc.
275 South Beverly Drive
Beverly Hills, California 90212

SAGE Publications India Pvt. Ltd.
M-32 Market
Greater Kailash I
New Delhi 110 048 India

SAGE Publications Ltd
28 Banner Street
London EC1Y 8QE
England

Printed in the United States of America

Library of Congress Cataloging-in-Publication Data

Pope, Whitney
   Alexis de Tocqueville: his social and political theory.

   (Masters of social theory ; v. 4)
   Bibliography: p.
   Includes index.
   1. Tocqueville, Alexis de, 1805-1859.
I. Title. II. Series.
JC229.T8P65 1985   301'.092'4   85-19605
ISBN 0-8039-2556-5
ISBN 0-8039-2557-3 (pbk.)

FIRST PRINTING

Contents

To Sarah Haydock Pope

a humanitarian who inspires by her calm direction and ceaseless activity, which daily transform time into progress

Series Editor's Introduction

Alexis de Tocqueville is often ignored in analyses of the early masters of sociological theory. He was, in a sense, a philosopher, historian, political scientist, and sociologist; and as a consequence, no one discipline can make an exclusive claim on him. Moreover, he wrote his most important works before sociology was well established as an academic discipline with the result that he is sometimes obscured by the long shadows of Durkheim, Marx, and Weber. Yet, as Whitney Pope documents in the chapters of this fourth volume of the Sage Masters of Social Theory series, we would do well to reconsider Tocqueville. For more than is commonly recognized, his ideas have profoundly influenced contemporary social science.

To a greater extent than any scholar of his time, Tocqueville used systematic historical comparisons to isolate the impact of structural variables on fundamental social processes. True, he was a historian and fell prey to many of their biases, such as historiography, but he also used comparative methods to sort out the generic classes of variables in those fundamental processes that were changing the shape of societies—namely, the centralization of power and the breakdown of traditional class-status boundaries. As Pope emphasizes, Tocqueville implicitly presented formal causal models on the conditions promoting centralized power and equalization of status. This is, in my view, historical sociology at its best, for it rises above the particulars and tries to say something about fundamental processes in all social systems.

There is also a moral-philosophical tone in all of Tocqueville's work. He was concerned about freedom, democracy, and equality in a world where power, authority, and community must also exist. His theory is, as Pope emphasizes, one that analyzes simultaneously the moral questions of "freedom-tyranny, community-egoism, decentralized-centralized administration, and authority-force." More than most social philosophers, however, Tocqueville translates these philosophical concerns and their analysis in the historical record into interesting theoretical propositions and models. Pope does an excellent job of demonstrating how Tocqueville can make this translation without diluting either the philosophical or theoretical portions of his work.

Laguna Beach, California   —*Jonathan H. Turner*

Acknowledgments

For the second time in writing a book, I owe my greatest intellectual debt to Barclay Johnson. Intending to coauthor a book on Tocqueville, we spent a summer discussing him. Though geographical separation and other problems prevented us from realizing our intention, Johnson's ideas and those developed during our conversations have greatly influenced my thinking. I have also profited from innumerable enjoyable discussions with Timothy Tilton. An Indiana University Summer Faculty Fellowship allowed me to spend one summer working on this book. Both authors appreciate the reactions to our work of those who have read part or all of it: Jere Cohen, Randall Collins, Walter Nugent, Charles Powers, Steven Stack, Tendzin Takla, and Steve Warner. Thanks also go to Maurice Garnier, who read the entire manuscript and advised me on translations; to Frank Burleigh, for assistance with word processing; and to Delanie, Whitney, and Braxton Pope for computer and library assistance. I cannot imagine writing a book without the intellectual and other assistance provided by Christie Farnham Pope, assistance that certainly impeded realization of her own professional goals. Finally, the dedication reflects the admiration of two generations for a third.

1

Tocqueville's Reception in Contemporary Social Science

A self-proclaimed liberal, but "of a new kind" (Tocqueville, 1862, 1: 381), who, seeking "new remedies for new ills," proposed to develop "a new political science . . . for a world itself quite new" (Tocqueville, 1835, 1840/1969: 701, 12; see also 302), Alexis de Tocqueville has been labeled an aristocratic apologist (Parsons, 1968: xiv), a conservative (Lukacs, 1968: 14; Smelser and Warner, 1976: 38), a conservative liberal (Hoffmann, 1982: 38), a liberal (Pierson, 1938: 47; Schapiro, 1942; Talmon, 1960a: 257; Drescher, 1964a: 1-17; Aron, 1967: vii; Nisbett, 1975: 247; Halebsky, 1976: 21; Tilton, 1979), a Frenchman whose nationalism sometimes subverted his liberalism (Richter, 1963), and even a conservative Marxist (Salomon, 1960: 458). Lukacs (1982: 7-8) feels that the "unclassifiable" Tocqueville transcends the liberal and conservative labels, and Lively (1962: 8) argues that these labels are equally artificial, because "a case could as easily be made out for one as for the other." Indeed, Tocqueville's "contributions to the ideologies of both Liberalism and Conservatism are now taken for granted" (White, 1973: 193) as representatives of both have claimed him as one of their own.

Salomon (1962: 263-81), Shils (1961: 1418), and Gargan (1965: 14-15) call him a moralist, and Drescher (1964a: viii) a publicist. He has been identified as an anthropologist (Mayer, 1966b: viii), a legal historian (Mayer, 1966b: viii), a philosopher (Pierson, 1938: 756; Schapiro, 1942: 545; Salomon, 1962: 282-309; Gargan, 1965: 14-15; Smith, 1981: 146), "the most profound philosopher of the modern democratic age" (Gargan, 1965: 15), and the "great prophet of the Mass Age," (Mayer, 1966a: xv). Most frequently, Tocqueville is seen as a historian, sociologist, political scientist, philosopher, and social and political theorist. Tocqueville himself (1862, 2: 252) viewed his own work as a mixture of science, history, and philosophy.

Amid these diverse labelings Tocqueville's genius is widely acknowledged (Beaumont in Tocqueville, 1862, 1: 42, Beloff, 1962: 171; Berlin, 1965: 205; Eberts and Witton, 1970: 1095; Nisbet, 1975: 198, 1977: 75; Stinchcombe, 1978: 5). His work is acute (Drescher, 1980: 468), powerful (Halebsky, 1976: 22), seminal (Halebsky, 1976: 21), shrewd (Lerner, 1966: xxvi), illuminating (Bendix, 1977: 37, 61), penetrating (Richter, 1963: 362, Bendix, 1978: 340), brilliant (Baltzell, 1964: 9, Horowitz, 1967: 269; Stinchcombe, 1978: 46), profound (Wolin, 1960: 349), sensitive (Lerner, 1966: xxvi), incisive (Smelser, 1976: 36), and, above all, insightful (Bendix, 1962: 462, Lerner, 1966: xxvi; Furet, 1981: 132, 161) and prescient (Commager, 1950: 365; Riesman, 1950: 166; Nef, 1963: 474; Nisbet, 1975: 128; Halebsky, 1976: 23). Tocqueville had "an extraordinary range of observation and an awesome depth of perception" (Inkeles, 1979: 393). His work demonstrates a powerful sociological imagination (Weitman, 1966: 389). *Democracy in America* (1835, 1840/1969; hereafter cited as *Democracy*) is widely regarded as the finest study of American culture and society (Taub, 1974: 5), and, indeed, as "one of the most brilliant and penetrating studies of a civilization ever written" (Pessen, 1978: 77) if not "the greatest on any national polity and culture" (Lerner, 1966: xxv). *The Old Regime and the French Revolution* (1856/1955; hereafter cited as *The Old Regime*) is not only the classic analysis of France's old regime and the causes of the French Revolution but is "possibly the greatest historical book ever written" (Collins and Makowsky, 1978: 62).

Tocqueville is often included among the preeminent social, political, and historical thinkers. Riesman (1950: 178) cites the "great tradition of modern political science that runs from Machiavelli and Hobbes to Tocqueville and Marx." Next to Marx, writes Lerner (1966: lxxxiii), Tocqueville is "the greatest historian and political sociologist of the last century." Collins (1975: 527) considers Tocqueville and Marx "the greatest of the nineteenth-century social thinkers." Mayer (1966a: xv), and Wilhelm Dilthey (quoted in Nisbet, 1977: 59), respectively, view Tocqueville as "probably the most important sociologist of the nineteenth century," and as "the greatest analyst of the political world since Machiavelli and Aristotle."

Salomon (1960: 463) identifies Tocqueville as "the founder of a sociology of politics," and Lipset (1963: 12) adds the names of Marx,

Weber, and Michels in identifying the four people who have done the most to define contemporary political sociology. Lerner (1966: x1) contends that "Tocqueville almost single-handedly shaped a political sociology, a military sociology, a sociology of the intellectual life, a theory of alienation, a theory of mass culture and mass tyranny in a democracy." Beyond his often cited contributions to political sociology, Stone and Mennell (1980: 24) observe that Tocqueville contributed "to the sociology of social stratification, race relations, slavery, colonialism, communities, voluntary associations, bureaucracies, armies, language, literature, art, religion, prisons, and crime. He even discussed the social position of women. . . . He was indeed a well-rounded sociologist."

His insight, breadth, and literary style make Tocqueville an endless source of quotations. "Of all the great unread writers," observes humorist Russell Baker (1976: 33), "I believe de Tocqueville to be the most widely quoted." In addition to the quotes that are liberally distributed throughout works on a range of topics, he is conspicuous as the author of the prominently displayed quote. Tocqueville remains a favorite source for book (Hartz, 1955; Kornhauser, 1959; Palmer, 1959; Talmon, 1960a, 1960b; Probst, 1962; Baltzell, 1964; Wood, 1969), and chapter (Riesman, 1950: 148, 177, 256, 271, 368; Baltzell, 1964: 197, 260; 1979: 179, 335, 369) epigraphs, chapter openings (Aron, 1968: 66; Baltzell, 1979: 281, 417) and closings (Aron, 1968: 85-88), and book beginnings (Smith and Freedman, 1972: v) and conclusions (Masaryk 1881/1970: 231; White, 1954: 567; Palmer, 1964: 573-75).

Insofar as Tocqueville is linked to specific themes, the perceived value of his work rises and falls with the currency of those ideas and the general perspectives with which they are associated. When studies of American national character—for example, Almond's *The American People and Foreign Policy* (1950), Riesman's *The Lonely Crowd* (1950) and Potter's *People of Plenty* (1954)—and the theme of American conformity were current, Tocqueville was culled for observations on American national character (for example, Whyte, 1956: 5,395) and the "tyranny of the majority." (For an example of Tocqueville's influence on recent thinking about American national character see Inkeles, 1979).

Another source of Tocqueville's renewed prominence in the 1950s and early 1960s was the consensus school (for example, Boorstin, 1953; Hartz, 1955) and pluralist-mass society theory analyses of American history and society. Kornhauser's (1959: 25, passim) well-known statement of this theory is indebted to him. In the best-known overview of political sociology, Lipset (1963: 1-24) treats Tocqueville as a pluralist and locates in his work a stress on both voluntary associations and local self-government as institutions perpetuating the consensus and structural pluralism necessary for a free democracy (Lipset, 1963: 7-8). A major study of Lipset et al. (1956) uses Tocqueville's work to supplement and extend Michels's work, thereby specifying the conditions promoting or precluding the outcome described in Michels's (1915/ 1959) iron law of oligarchy. Emphasizing Michels more than Tocqueville, *Union Democracy* only begins to trace its links to the latter. Consequently, its indebtedness to Tocqueville is widely overlooked. Nonetheless, *Union Democracy* remains the best empirically based, contemporary analysis of the relations among Tocqueville's central variables of community, pluralism (decentralized administration), liberty, and authority.

As symbolized in the similarity of its title to that of Tocqueville's (1969) major work on America, Dahl's political science textbook, *Democracy in the United States*, is very Tocquevillian. Dahl (1976: 53-59) identifies five distinguishing characteristics of the American polyarchy, each of which was previously analyzed by Tocqueville: (1) discrimination against racial minorities; (2) equality: ideal versus reality, (3) wide acceptance of American institutions; (4) extreme partitioning of political authority; and (5) incrementalist perspectives on political action. Dahl (1976: 97-101, 106-107, 113-114, 119) cites Tocqueville in support of his thesis that two of these—equality and ideological agreement—were particularly decisive in the development of the American polyarchy.

The pluralist-consensus components in Tocqueville and his influence on Dahl and other pluralists created a widespread perception of Tocqueville as "the historical progenitor" of consensus theory (Horowitz, 1967: 269). As poverty, racism, sexism, war and peace, American imperialism, and international political economy became the major concerns in the 1960s and 1970s, these perspectives were increasingly supplanted by competing viewpoints; and Tocqueville's popularity seemed to fade along with the consensus-pluralist perspectives with which he had become identified.

The breadth of Tocqueville's work, however, encouraged recognition of its relevance for emerging concerns. After World War II America was the dominant world power. Formerly incorporated into European empires, Asian and African societies struggled for and achieved national independence. These developments provided the context for a renewed American interest in comparative-historical studies, particularly of modernization. Bendix (1977: 37-126; 1978: 321-77) combines Tocquevillian and Weberian perspectives to study "the great transformation" in Western Europe, and Huntington (1968) uses Tocqueville's ideas to study development, lack of development, and stability/instability in both the developed nations and those currently seeking to develop.

As consensus, pluralist, and functionalist perspectives waned in the late sixties and seventies, the conflict perspective waxed. Increasing emphasis on conflict in history and society has heightened concern with collective protest and revolution. Skocpol's (1979: 6-14) discussion of four important families of theories of revolution does not cite Tocqueville as a decisive influence on any of them; rather, she simply mentions him along with Durkheim and Weber as a classical antecedent of contemporary theories of revolution (Skocpol, 1979: 8). However, Piven and Cloward (1979: 8) identify the contrasting views of Marx and Tocqueville as the two most influential general perspectives on revolution, the former holding that revolutions are most likely to occur as conditions improve, the latter as conditions worsen. Davies's (1962) J-curve theory of revolution combines their views. In the most comprehensive recent statement of *Conflict Sociology*, Collins (1975: 528) identifies Tocqueville as an important progenitor of contemporary conflict theory and notes that like Marx he "began to formulate the principles of conflict and the organizational conditions determining its outcomes."

IS TOCQUEVILLE STILL RELEVANT?

A minority disputes Tocqueville's continued relevance. Generally, this conclusion is based on the perception that, reflecting his lack of interest in and consequent tendency to underplay the importance of economic factors (Spiller et al., 1974: 213; Goldstein, 1975: 123-124: Stone and Mennell, 1980: 35, 41), Tocqueville slighted the massive changes associated with the growth of the market and industrialization. By acknowledging but not emphasizing the importance of industrialization, Tocqueville "wrote in parentheses what was to be the bold type of the next century's history" (Lively, 1962: 217). Tocqueville's great weakness, writes Tilton (1979: 284-285), is that his theory is "intended for, and [is] more applicable to, agricultural or commercial societies, not modern industrial societies."

On the other hand, numerous scholars assert Tocqueville's continued, if not increased, relevance (for example, Berlin, 1965: 200; Pierson, 1980: xvi). Nisbet (1968: 93) points out that Tocqueville "was keenly aware of the social impact of the new industrialism. This is why he emphasized the money base of social stratification of the new democratic society and why he studied such matters as technology, division of labor, wages, land rents, and cyclical business depression." Though Pierson (1938: 175, 762-765) criticized Tocqueville for his neglect of industrialization and other economic forces, later his Foreword (1980: xvii) to Schleifer acknowledges the latter's demonstration that "Tocqueville paid considerably more attention to the American economy than I and others have supposed." Schleifer (1980: 168; see also p. 171) notes that, though the published version of *Democracy* emphasized industrialization less than the trend toward equality, the book's working manuscript "for a time boldly ranked the industrial revolution with the advance of *démocratie* [equality] as the two great social developments of modern Western culture." Furthermore, by 1838 Tocqueville "was persuaded that industrialization and increasing equality were the two great forces of the times." Accordingly, he "explored the ways in which industry, centralization, and *démocratie* strengthened one another and moved relentlessly ahead together" (Schleifer, 1980: 283-284). Schapiro (1942: 560) is astonished that Tocqueville "visualized the problems raised by modern industrialism as far back as the thirties of the nineteenth century, when it was in its infancy in both France and America."

Democracy "is a powerful work that still seems fresh today," and Tocqueville's predictions remain cogent (Bell, 1976: 8, 318). Commenting on Riesman's (1950) analysis of contemporary American social character, Dahrendorf (1961: 176) argues that the similarity of their conclusions makes *The Lonely Crowd* "a continuous dispute between Mr. Riesman and Tocqueville about who said (and meant) what first." Lerner (1966: xlvi) writes that "an American of the mid-1960's, reading *Democracy* today, has the uncanny feeling of reading not about Jackson's America but of his own," whereas Taub (1974: 7) observes that today *Democracy* is often read as a description of "*contemporary* American life." Mayer (1966a: 37) feels that "after the passage of a hundred years" Tocqueville's account of "What Sort of Despotism Democratic Nations Have to Fear" (Tocqueville, 1969: 690-695) has "proved an exact description of a present-day reality" (fascism). For Lerner (1966: xxv), *Democracy's* "influence is greater than ever, its relevance to the needs of the day deeper."

Winthrop (1981: 91) considers *The Old Regime* to be "as worthy of attention" now as when first published. Tocqueville's "analysis of French politics," writes Aron (1965: 210), is "exceptionally lucid. It may be applied to the whole political history of France in the nineteenth and twentieth centuries." Furthermore, (Aron, 1965: 192) of the visions of Comte, Marx, and Tocqueville, Tocqueville's "most closely resembles Western European societies today."

Though initially *The Power Elite* (1959: 226-227) questioned Tocqueville's contemporary relevance, later it (1959: 301) identifies him as among the first to see a major trend of modern society, "the transformation of public into mass." Collins and Makowsky (1978: 52) refer to his "timeless viewpoint on the dangers of power . . . [that] has kept him contemporary and relevant," Bendix (1962: 462) points to his "insight

into the totalitarian potential of democracy [that] astonishes us today,"
and Nisbet (1962: 191) to Tocqueville's analysis of totalitarianism that
"has not been improved upon by even the most brilliant of contemporary students of the subject." "It is only in our time," adds Nisbet
(1975: 198), that Tocqueville's analysis of the affinity between equality
and the centralization of power has "become analytic and descriptive
rather than prophetic." Lukacs (1982: 7) finds Tocqueville's vision
"startlingly applicable to the historical and social conditions of our own
times."

TOCQUEVILLE AS SCIENTIST AND THEORIST

Tocqueville's Approach and Treatment Of Data

Commentators have long debated whether Tocqueville's work is
scientific, inductive, adequately grounded in the data, and based on
careful research or whether, in contrast, it is nonscientific by virtue of
being a priori, deductive, inadequately grounded empirically, and based
upon inadequate research methods. Current disagreements about the
scientific status of Tocqueville's work perpetuate the evaluations stated
long ago by James Bryce (1887: 5-6, 22-57) and John Stuart Mill.
Identifying (Bryce, 1887: 23) three causes of the defects in *Democracy*,
one of which was that Tocqueville's "strong and penetrating intellect . . .
moved by preference in the *a priori* or deductive path, and his power of
observation. . . did not lead but followed the march of his reasonings,"
Bryce (1887: 28) concludes that "in spite of its scientific form, it
[*Democracy*] is really a work of art rather than a work of science."
Pierson (1938: 756-761) considers Tocqueville's method philosophical,
unscientific, and "vulnerability itself." Tocqueville relied too heavily on
generalization and abstraction and too little on systematic compilation
of the necessary empirical foundation. "The process of deduction from
deduction" was sometimes "carried so far that all connection with fact
and reality" was left behind and what began as a rational process
"wound up in purest nonsense" (Pierson, 1938: 760-761). In short, "the
vice of Tocqueville's method . . . was precisely its *unscientific* quality"
(Pierson, 1938: 760). In *Democracy*, argues Zeitlin (1971: 56), "Tocqueville wrote more as a philosopher of history and less as a methodologi-
cally rigorous and empirical historian or social scientist. He conceived a
great central historical law [trend toward equality] and proceeded
largely to deduce from that law everything that appeared logically to
follow." In contrast, in the second of his two famous reviews of

Democracy, volumes 1 and 2, Mill (1840/1962: 233), himself author of the classic work on scientific method, *A System of Logic* (Mill, 1884), calls Tocqueville's method "the true Baconian and Newtonian method applied to society and government." Mill (1962: 232) praises *Democracy* as "the beginning of a new era in the scientific study of politics." More than a century later Richter (1967: 77) asserts that "Tocqueville tended to generalize by first immersing himself in particular cases" and that (1969: 153) Tocqueville's explanations "did not depend upon deductions from general laws." Eberts and Witton (1970: 1089, 1081) commend Tocqueville's "creation of theory through rigorous observations (of both United States and European society), generalization, and abstraction" and development of "an impressive, theoretically based and empirically supported analytic model."

Tocqueville is seen both as prone to asserting and suspicious of general laws. In contrast to Smelser's (1976: 36; see also Richter, 1969: 153) contention that Tocqueville was "generally hostile to" such laws is White's (1973: 193) assertion that Tocqueville "studied history in order to determine the causal laws that govern its operations." Perhaps, however, the sharpest differences of opinion concern data. Smelser (1976: 30) cites "the qualitative and impressionistic nature" of Tocqueville's data, and Bryce (1887: 23) feels that "the facts he cites are rather the illustrations than the sources of his conclusions." Nonetheless, Martindale (1960: 39) identifies Tocqueville's work as among the first to exemplify "a new kind of analysis, the detailed empirical examination of political phenomena in the rich context of social factors giving rise to them," thereby dramatizing "the rich rewards to be gained by empirical study." Similarly, Taub (1974: 17) views *Democracy* as "one of the great empirical social scientific studies of the 19th century."

Tocqueville has been accused of allowing his preconceptions to cause him to perceive selectively, distort, or even ignore relevant data. Bryce (1887: 25) feels that Tocqueville "is struck by those [facts] which accord with" and is "apt to ignore those which diverge from his preconceptions." "In the grip of a preconceived idea [America was the land of universal equality]," states Pierson (1938: 164), Tocqueville and Beaumont "were fitting the facts observed in the United States to a conviction about America brought with them from France." Once Tocqueville decided on an explanation, "he tended to gather only those facts that fitted his theory" (Pierson, 1938: 759). Commager (1946: xvi) adds that Tocqueville "tended to substitute his own reflections for facts, or, where the facts were stubborn, to force them into his own preconceived pattern." Tocqueville "saw in America what he wished to see," writes Zeitlin (1971: 58), "and either ignored or treated as exceptional all phenomena not in accord with his master concept" ("of an already equalitarian

America growing ever more equalitarian"; Zeitlin, 1971: 57). "Thus Tocqueville deceived himself." (Compare Richter, 1963: 362: Tocqueville was one of the "least deceived political theorists of the nineteenth century.")

Others defend Tocqueville. Qualifying his earlier assessment, Bryce (1887: 25) notes that Tocqueville "is admirably honest, never conceding or consciously evading a fact which he perceives might tell against his theories." "He had no desire to prove or disprove any theory or system. He had no preconceived idea or prejudice, but as a judge he had been trained to look for the evidence and the facts of a case" (Spiller et al., 1974: 210). Marshall and Drescher (1968: 527) observe Tocqueville's refusal "to force his analysis into a tight system, which would be consistent with a priori beliefs." As "testimony to de Tocqueville's seriousness as a historian," Stinchcombe (1978: 46) cites his preference to contradict himself rather "than not report the facts as he sees them."

In contrast to those who question the adequacy of Tocqueville's data and research methods, Collins (1975: 539) lauds his "meticulous historical research," Schapiro (1942: 549) his "careful research," and Schleifer (1980: 275) his thorough research. And in the midst of disagreement otherwise, Tocqueville's comparative method is seen as exemplary (for a dissenting view see Pierson, 1938: 758). Indeed, the author of *Political Man* (Lipset, 1963: 24) "suggests that the sociology of politics return to the problem posed by Tocqueville: the social requisites and consequences of democracy," a focus which "forces us to the method he employed so successfully: comparative analysis." Skocpol (1979: 36) describes "the method of comparative historical *analysis*—in which the overriding intent is to develop, test, and refine causal, explanatory hypotheses about events or structures integral to macro-units such as nation-states." This "method was applied to powerful effect by such classical social and historical analysts as Alexis de Tocqueville and Marc Bloch." Collins (1975: 5) emphasizes the importance of comparative studies designed to establish the general causes of variation: "The classic comparisons by Tocqueville and Weber, or more recent comparative studies such as those of Gerhard Lenski (1966) and Barrington Moore (1966), have done far more to set forth the principles of political and economic structure than any number of more precise investigations that lack either comparative scope or a serious theoretical perspective."

Tocqueville as Theorist

Subject to varying evaluation, Tocqueville's place in contemporary social science and sociology is far from secure. At the extreme are those who deny that he is a historian (Pierson, 1938: 756) or social scientist (Pierson, 1938: 756; Coser, 1977: 322). More typically, Tocqueville is ignored or mentioned only in passing. For example, Park and Burgess's influential *Introduction to the Science of Sociology* (1921/1969) mentions Tocqueville only twice. Nor has Tocqueville always fared better in the post-World War II period. Devoting entire chapters to such notables as Hans Freyer, Jacques Novicow, Guillame de Greef, Benjamin Kidd, and Mariano Cornejo, Barnes's lengthy *An Introduction to the History of Sociology* includes no reference to Tocqueville. The *Handbook of Modern Sociology* (Faris, 1964: 841) refers to him but once.

Like that of most other sociologists who died some time ago, Tocqueville's reception in contemporary social science depends largely on the evaluation of his theoretical contributions. Thus his reception as a theorist parallels his reception in sociology, generally. A long-standing tradition denies Tocqueville a place among the great thinkers simply by ignoring him. Sorokin's (1928: 720) *Contemporary Sociological Theories* and Barnes and Becker's *Social Thought from Lore to Science* (1938: 564) each contain but one passing reference to Tocqueville. Innumerable theory texts or books on theory fail to mention Tocqueville (Giddens, 1971; Timasheff and Theodorson, 1976; Cuzzort and King, 1980; Ritzer, 1983; Wilson, 1983), briefly quote or mention him in passing (Coser, 1977: 322; Wallace and Wolf, 1980: 199-200; Martindale, 1981: 417, 589-590; Rhea, 1981: 12, 42, 50), or relegate him to a footnote (Rossides, 1978: 378n; Johnson, 1981: 199). One text (Turner 1978: ix) includes "discussion of all the major historical figures in sociology" but fails to mention Tocqueville. *The Emergence of Sociological Theory* (Turner and Beeghley, 1981: 324-328, 331-332) briefly treats Tocqueville but only in the context of his presumed influence on Durkheim.

When sociologists are most self-conscious about theory, Tocqueville's name may not come up (for example, Alexander, 1982). Readers of books on the nature of theory and theory construction in sociology will not be surprised to find discussion of *Suicide* (Durkheim, 1897/1951), specifically Durkheim's proposition that Catholics have lower suicide rates than Protestants (Merton, 1957: 96-98; Stinchcombe, 1968: 15-27, 32-33; Wallace, 1971: 25-29; Gibbs, 1972: 105-06; Winton, 1974: 24-26). The same readers may look in vain, however, for illustrative use of Tocqueville's work in discussions of the art of theorizing (Stinchcombe, 1968; Wallace, 1971; Winton, 1974). Gibbs's (1972: 9) single reference to Tocqueville cites him as an example of a grand theorist whose work, even more than that of the other grand theorists, Marx, Durkheim, Pareto, and Weber, is the antithesis of the formal theory construction advocated by Gibbs. The goal of those who engage in the "ancestor worship" of Tocqueville and other grand theorists "is not theory construction (formal or otherwise) but 'scholarly works.' For them, the method and aspirations of Tocqueville are forever sufficient." Although the hasty reader might conclude that there is more to be learned about theorizing from Durkheim's analysis of Protestant and Catholic suicide rates than from anything in Tocqueville, Richter (1969) and Smelser (1976: 6-37) analyze Tocqueville's comparative method and Stinchcombe (1978: 31-76) compares the theoretical methods of Tocqueville and Trotsky.

Parsons is one of the few scholars denying Tocqueville the status of a major theorist who justifies his denial. The "Introduction to the paperback edition" explains why the first edition of *The Structure of Social Action* (Parsons, 1937/1968) contains no reference to Tocqueville. Among those in the phase preceding Weber and Durkheim, Marx and Tocqueville were the most important thinkers (Parsons, 1968: xiii). However, "*all* the theoretical endeavors before the generation of Durkheim and Max Weber" were merely "proto-sociology" (Parsons, 1954: 349). Though insightful, Tocqueville "was much more an extremely talented 'commentator' on the social and political scene, than the originator of major theoretical schemes for analysis" (Parsons, 1967: 641). A talented essayist (Parsons, 1968: xivn), Tocqueville was not a great theorist. Parsons's denial that Tocqueville, Marx, or any other predecessor of Durkheim and Weber was a theorist suggests his own idiosyncratic understanding of theory. Certainly, Parsons is vague about why none of these men is a theorist.

Parsons's sometimes coauthor and coeditor Shils (1961: 1447) makes a parallel assessment. Identifying the work of Weber, Durkheim, Tonnies, and Scheler as classics of modern sociology, Shils denies Tocqueville similar status. Citing only *Democracy* and making no mention of *The Old Regime* or other works by Tocqueville, Shils does observe that, like a number of other important works, Tocqueville's is a work of "analytical scholarship and reflective observation" that retains "a freshness and pertinence to contemporary sociological analysis . . . because we have not exceeded them." The great sociologists, Tocqueville included, "had more insight and understanding of fundamental things than practically any living sociologist, and their ideas have not yet been widely absorbed." Given such an eloquent appraisal, perhaps even the Tocqueville partisan will remain content. Shils is far clearer about Tocqueville's merits than what it is about his work that fails to qualify it as a classic of modern sociology.

Smelser (1976: 6-37) argues that Tocqueville only verged on stating theory. Like Parsons, Smelser (1976: 36) characterizes Tocqueville as "mainly an incisive commentator," and denies that he was a theorist. "Yet . . . a conceptual organization—however incomplete—emerges from his observations and insights." Smelser (1976: 35) discerns in Tocqueville a "semi-developed model of interacting historical causes" and a "nascent theoretical system."

Analyzing (Smelser, 1976: 7; emphasis added) "Tocqueville's two classic works—*Democracy in America* and *The Old Regime and the French Revolution*—as a single study in comparative sociological explanation,* Smelser (1976: 11-22) treats such topics as "Tocqueville's explanation of the differences between France and America" (Smelser, 1976: 11) and identifies (1976: 23) the causal relations in "Tocqueville's model [of the French Revolution] of 'circumstances remote in time and of a general order.' " Smelser addresses Tocqueville's causal model (but not theory?) of the occurrence of the French Revolution and Tocqueville's "sociological explanation," generally. Indeed, laced throughout his discussion are references to Tocqueville's propositions, models, causal framework, and explanatory principles. Smelser analyzes the very theory the existence of which he denies.

If some ignore him as a theorist or deny the existence of his theory,[1] others deem Tocqueville one of sociology's first theoreticians (Aron, 1966: 201);[2] a theoretical genius (Eberts and Witton, 1970: 1095); a grand theorist (Richter, 1970: 102); a great theorist (Richter, 1970: 76; Bell, 1976: 318n); and a consummate theorist (Weitman, 1966: 389). His theory is powerful (Collins and Makowsky, 1978: 60), a lasting contribution (Smelser and Warner, 1976: 38), fully developed (Richter, 1970: 101), and well thought out (Stone and Mennell, 1980: 25).

There are as many different classifications of Tocqueville as a theorist as there are such classifications. Lipset's (1963: 4-12) approach, treating Marx and Tocqueville as conflict and consensus theorists, and Weber and Michels as theorists of bureaucracy and democracy, is faulty in that Tocqueville was centrally concerned with the relationship between centralization (bureaucratization) and democracy. Aron (1965: 259-260) places the four theorists treated in the first volume of *Main Currents in Sociological Thought* in three schools. Montesquieu and Tocqueville are in the French school of political sociology. The second includes Comte and culminates in Durkheim and "the official and licensed sociologists of today," and the third is Marxist. Aron character-

---

1. Tocqueville's reception as a political thinker has been as uneven as his reception as a sociological theorist; he is ignored (Bluhm, 1978; Germino, 1972; Sibley, 1970; Sabine, 1961), mentioned in passing (Wolin, 1960: 271-272, 349, 417), and treated as one of the greats (Ebenstein, 1957: 464-500; 1969: 532-540, 547-563; Strauss and Cropsey, 1972: 715-736).

2. Even Aron (1965: 183) expresses uncertainty about theory in Tocqueville: "Tocqueville's theory, if we may call it that." Later in the same work Aron (1965: 230-231) does speak of theory in Tocqueville.

izes these schools as cautious, optimistic, and utopian, respectively. Collins (1968) classifies Weber, Tocqueville, Hintze, and Fustel de Coulanges as historical and comparative sociologists (1968: 43, 47) in contrast to structural-functionalists such as Parsons and Durkheim. Designed to emphasize the difference between Weber and Durkheim (Collins, 1968: 48), this classification makes the placement of Marx problematic. A footnote (Collins, 1968: 56n) distinguishes between functionalist and Marxist social-system models. The classification is misleading in that it implicitly denies the historical and comparative dimensions that pervade Durkheim, Marx, and the later Parsons (for example, 1966, 1971). In Collins's (1975: 20-22, 56-61, 527-528) subsequent classification Marx crosses the boundary to join Machiavelli, Hobbes, Weber, and Tocqueville as conflict theorists in contrast to such systems theorists as Comte, Pareto, Durkheim, and Parsons. Eberts and Witton (1970: 1089-1090) state that if, as they feel he should be, "Tocqueville could be considered a forefather of sociology, he stands much more in the tradition of Durkheim and Weber" than do Comte and Spencer.

Since the early sixties, recognition of Tocqueville's theoretical contribution has increased.[3] In *Main Currents in Sociological Thought*, Aron (1965: 183) writes, "Tocqueville is not ordinarily included among the founders of sociology; I consider this neglect of Tocqueville's sociological writings unjustified." Aron's two-volume work devotes a section to each of seven sociologists including Tocqueville (the others: Montesquieu, Comte, Marx, Durkheim, Pareto, and Weber). *The Sociological Tradition* (Nisbet ,1966: viii; see also Nisbet, 1968: 94) identifies Tocqueville, Marx, Tonnies, Weber, Durkheim, and Simmel as the thinkers who have done "the most to give systematic shape to modern sociological theory." Furthermore, "the sociological tradition may indeed be seen as a kind of magnetic field with Tocqueville and Marx as the two poles of attraction. In the long run the influence of Tocqueville on the sociological tradition has been the greater." Elsewhere, Nisbet (1968: 94) asserts that Tocqueville's

> distinction between power, class, and status and his emphasis upon the mass potential of modern democracy, upon administrative centralization, and upon the mass character of modern culture supplied the theoretical background for the more detailed and systematic treatments of these

---

3. Tocqueville is also regarded highly by some historians. For instance, those concerned with Jacksonian America often use *Democracy* as a resource (White, 1954; Meyers, 1957). Illustrating the quotable Tocqueville, Smith's (1981: 146-162) chapter on "Tocqueville's America" contains about as much material written by Tocqueville as by Smith. Nonetheless, Tocqueville is not the model for historians to the degree that Marx, Weber, and Durkheim are or even Tocqueville himself is for some nonhistorians.

forces that flourished in the sociology of France, Italy, and Germany at the end of the century. Burckhardt, Taine, Le Play, Acton, Tonnies, Weber, Simmel, and Michels all employed perspectives based on Tocqueville.[4]

In *Images of Society*, Poggi (1972) treats three authors: Tocqueville, Marx, and Durkheim. Similarly, Warner (Smelser and Warner, 1976) devotes entire chapters to Tocqueville, Marx, Durkheim, and Weber. Tocqueville is also the subject of one chapter in *The Discovery of Society* (Collins and Makowsky, 1978). Whether by explicit characterization or by the company he keeps, Tocqueville is increasingly identified as one of the giants along with, most frequently, Marx, Durkheim, and Weber.

As author of numerous works in several languages on Tocqueville (for example Mayer, 1966a), editor of English translations of Tocqueville (for example, Tocqueville, 1966), and editor of the definitive edition of Tocqueville's *Oeuvres Complètes* (Tocqueville, 1951), Mayer has done much to increase scholarly appreciation of Tocqueville. Aron is widely credited with the general resurgence of interest in Tocqueville, and the University of California, Berkeley, has been a fountainhead of Tocquevillian scholarship. The majority of those who collectively have done the most to promote recognition of his work have been associated with Berkeley's sociology department either as faculty, including Bendix, Nisbet, Lipset, Kornhauser, and Smelser, or as students, including Collins, Makowsky, Poggi, and Warner, and, in the case of Stinchcombe, both. Nisbet has long championed Tocqueville and Bendix, in addition to being personally linked with the Berkeley sociologists who have written about Tocqueville, has long used and developed his perspectives.

A number of articles and book chapters by Richter (1963, 1967, 1969, 1970) nominate him as the leading Tocquevillian scholar in political science. In history, the doyen (Goldstein, 1975: xi) of American Tocqueville scholars, Pierson, has contributed a classic tome on

---

4. In general, the authors cited by Nisbet fail to reveal Tocqueville's influence on them explicitly. For instance, none of the following cites Tocqueville: *Economy and Society* (Weber, 1968); *From Max Weber* (Weber, 1958a); *Community and Society* (Tonnies, 1957); *The Sociology of Georg Simmel* (Simmel, 1950). *Political Parties* (Michels, 1959: 13, 49) mentions Tocqueville twice. Going beyond Nisbet's list of authors, *The Division of Labor in Society* (Durkheim, 1960: 43-44) quotes one sentence from Tocqueville. Neither *Professional Ethics and Civic Morals* (Durkheim, 1958) nor *The Elementary Forms of the Religious Life* (Durkheim, 1965) mention him. The longer of two brief references to Tocqueville in *The Marx-Engels Reader* (Marx and Engels, 1972: 29, 498) is a reference by Marx in "The Eighteenth Brumaire of Louis Bonaparte" not to Tocqueville the social scientist but to Tocqueville the politician. Tocqueville appears to enter contemporary sociology directly and only secondarily as an important influence on other classic authors. In any case, Nisbet's assertion of his influence has yet to be documented and assessed.

Tocqueville and Beaumont in America (1938; abridged edition, 1968). More recently, Drescher (1964, 1968a) and Gargan (1955, 1965) have each authored two books in addition to other writings on Tocqueville (for example, Gargan 1959, 1962, 1963; Drescher, 1964b; Drescher, 1980; Marshall and Drescher, 1968) and editing of his works (Tocqueville and Beaumont, 1968).

Though Tocqueville is increasingly regarded as an exemplary sociologist, most of the contemporary books about him are authored by historians, or, less frequently, by political scientists. The British political scientist, Lively, wrote *The Social and Political Thought of Alexis de Tocqueville*, which remains an invaluable treatment of the man and his ideas. Although sociologists have translated and edited the works of Weber, Durkheim, Marx, Simmel, Pareto, and Tonnies, in Tocqueville's case this task has generally been done by historians and political scientists. Only belatedly was Tocqueville (1980) included in the Chicago Heritage of Sociology series.

The following chapters seek to resolve some of the continuing debates about Tocqueville. The most important issue, of course, is whether Tocqueville is a theorist and, if so, just what his theory is. The best way to resolve this dispute is by identifying his theory. My analysis of Tocqueville's theory of freedom is intended to promote the recognition, use, and development of one of social science's most valuable yet frequently slighted theoretical resources.

2

Tocqueville's Social and Political Theory

EXPLANATION IN HISTORY AND SOCIETY

Tocqueville (1862, 2: 31; 1836: 88) refers to "the general laws which govern human institutions" and those that "govern the universe" and asserts (1836: 81) that all phenomena "are subject to fixed laws, which it is not, perhaps, impossible to discover." *Democracy* (1969: 493-496, 439-441, 486) contrasts two approaches to explanation in history and society. Aristocratic historians attribute events to secondary causes, particularly the variable attributes of the powerful, such as their character and motives. In contrast, asserting the relative insignificance of individual people, democratic historians generalize to deny their collective influence. This leads them to seek out such decisive general causes as race, geography, or the spirit of a civilization that simultaneously affect everyone.

If both general causes and particular influences are always important, Tocqueville observes, their relative importance changes. In democratic societies general causes explain more, particular influences less; in aristocratic ages the reverse is true. Historians of democratic society err not in emphasizing the importance of general causes, but only in denying the lesser influence of what individuals do. Focusing on the impact of individuals, aristocratic historians do not link great causes into determinate systems, because they see powerful individuals constantly changing history.

The more powerful and smaller in number they are, the easier it is to discern a necessary, inevitable, absolute connection among causes. The approach of democratic historians predisposes them to make a serious mistake: They integrate general causes into abstract theories that postulate inevitable outcomes (1969: 496). Forgoing concern with how a nation might have chosen a better path, democratic historians construct fatalistic, determinant systems in which events occur independently of human will and could not have happened otherwise.

Tocqueville's posthumous *Recollections* (1970: 62) reemphasizes his rejection of deterministic theories: "I hate all those absolute systems that make all the events of history depend on great causes linked together by the chain of fate." Denying the sheer inexplicability of some historical circumstances, such systems also fail to appreciate that many important historical phenomena are due either to accidental circumstances or to a complex of secondary causes that, defying human explanation, must be regarded as chance. Though itself presupposing conditions permitting its operation, chance produces "those impromptu events that surprise and terrify us."

Rejecting absolute systems as empirically unfaithful to historical causation, as a moralist and voluntarist Tocqueville had even stronger reasons for detesting them. People are conscious, thinking, moral beings who, within the limits imposed by circumstances, remain "strong and free" (1969: 705) and whose individual and collective fate ultimately "depends on what they want to be" (1968b: 229). In banishing individuals from the history of the human race (1970: 62), absolute systems deny their freedom to make moral choices and influence their own fate.

Tocqueville (for example, 1968b: 226-229) was concerned with the practical implications of philosophical and scientific doctrines. History acquires its ultimate value not as an end in itself, but in relation to other human values. Social science should help in the realization of authentic human values such as justice and virtue. For Tocqueville (1862, 1: 299-300), the greatest happiness lay in fulfulling duty. His particular commitment was to liberty, which he always loved "instinctively" (1862, 1: 380). He repeatedly asserted this concern, sometimes noting his unwavering commitment amid liberty's changing circumstances in France (1955: xii, xv). Identifying the defense of freedom as his "whole life's passion" (1970: 105, 65), late in his life he (1862, 1: 406) referred to himself as "an old superannuated lover of liberty."

According to Tocqueville, philosophers and social scientists who attempt to promote human values must come to grips with social trends as the context for the realization of those values. Tocqueville sought to show others, especially those opposed to equality, the outline of the future so that they would not waste energy fighting the inevitable trend toward democracy. However, his purpose was not thereby to encourage resignation to an inevitable fate; to the contrary, he wished to energize people by convincing them that by their choices they would determine whether the equality of the future was to be combined with freedom or servitude. In *Democracy* (1969: xiv, 18-19, 244-245, 315, 702) and elsewhere (1862, 2: 13-14), he indicates that the book's purpose was not just to satisfy curiosity but to promote understanding of the lessons useful in solving the greatest problem of the time: how Christian nations could reap democracy's benefits while avoiding its evils (1969: 311).

Often he (1862, 1: 376-378) stated his purpose more specifically in terms of France's political alignments where the decisive split between the proponents of morality, religion, and order and those of liberty and legal equality distressed him (1862, 1: 379-382). Demonstrating that all these "sacred" things were not only compatible but necessarily connected would be a monumental achievement (1862, 1: 380). He sought to convince the French that freedom, which itself presupposes respect for the law, is the best guarantee of morality and religion (1862, 1: 382).

Tocqueville hoped his work on America (1969) would increase his fellow countrymen's understanding of democracy. To those who idealized free democratic government he wanted to show that, notwithstanding its benefits, it lacked some of the idealized features they attributed to it and presupposed conditions of intelligence, morality, and religious belief that France must labor to attain before being able to establish a free republican government. To the enemies of democracy who equated it with destruction and anarchy he wanted to show the virtues of democratic government; that it could be combined with respect for rights, liberty, and religion; and that the choice was no longer between democracy and aristocracy but between the benefits of free democracy and the evils of democratic despotism.

While striving to make it scientifically accurate, Tocqueville (1955: xii; 1862, 2: 229; 1862, 1: 351) also intended *The Old Regime* to have a positive influence on thinking and behavior. Never losing sight of contemporary France, he sought to show the reader the conditions favorable and unfavorable to freedom and prosperity (1862, 2: 230).

Social science should elevate, not lower, humanity (1862, 2: 384). Tocqueville's (1969: 736-749) review, not of *Democracy in America,* but *On Democracy in Switzerland* criticizes its author (Cherbuliez) for simply denouncing democracy instead of showing how to improve it. He (1968b: 227-232, 270, 291-292; see also 1862, 2: 399-400) rejects Gobineau's racist doctrines because they would promote the degradation of groups defined as racially inferior. "What purpose," he writes Gobineau

(1968b: 228-229), "does it serve to persuade lesser peoples living in abject conditions of barbarism or slavery that, such being their racial nature, they can do nothing to better themselves, to change their habits, or to ameliorate their status?" In sum, "probably quite false," Gobineau's doctrines are "certainly very pernicious" (1968b: 227). They exemplify the all too prevalent contemporary thinking that holds that nations "are never their own masters and that they are bound to obey some insuperable and unthinking power, the product of preexisting facts, of race, or soil, or climate." The conclusion to *Democracy* (1969: 705) denounces such "false and cowardly doctrines which can only produce feeble men and pusillanimous nations." For Tocqueville social science is an analytic science the explanations of which must be assessed, not only against the evidence, but also in terms of their usefulness in promoting the realization of authentic human values.

Authors who discern a deterministic historical pattern often predict the future, for example, as a realization of what was immanent in the past; as a resolution of past conflict and contradiction; as the inevitable triumph of a region, race, group, or idea; or as the continuation of history's linear, cyclical, or other pattern. Tocqueville's projection of the democratic revolution into the future, as well as many of his other predictions (see, for example, 1969: 169, 363, 383, 407-413; 1955: xii-xiii, 1968b: 268), might seem contrary to his rejection of absolute systems and deterministic generalizations about the future. He realized, however, that history shows that none who witnessed the pivotal historical changes in Western Europe, for example, the rise of Christianity, the downfall of the Roman Empire, or the rise of feudalism were able to forsee the aftermath of these revolutionary changes. "Who, then, can affirm that any one social system is essential, and that another is impossible?" (1862, 2: 105; see also 1862, 1: 401). Tocqueville does not deny the possibility of some equally unexpected future revolution, nor does he claim powers of prediction surpassing those of earlier authors. He (1970: 76; see also 1968b: 166) is wary of functionalist explanations that explain existence by an appeal to necessity. Rather, the vast diversity in human institutions tempts Tocqueville "to the belief that what are called necessary institutions are only institutions to which one is accustomed, and that in matters of social constitution the field of possibilities is much wider than people living within each society imagine." He (1955: xi; see also 1862, 1: 401) notes that the future of nations is often unpredictable, sees (1862, 2: 383) a black horizon limiting our view of the future, and, consistent with his views about causation in history, observes (1969: 357; see also 411; 1862, 1: 401) that the blind spot created by chance forever closes a part of the future to the mind's eye.

Despite these limitations, Tocqueville feels that generalizations about the past, present, and future are basic to social science. A careful, informed approach to the future helps people realize its benefits while avoiding its dangers. Tocqueville's assessment of the future is intended as just such a guide. His prediction of an egalitarian future is not framed as a metaphysical, suprahistorical assertion. Rather, it is empirical, subject to correction as the future unfolds, falsifiable, and carefully drawn on the basis of considerable evidence (see, for example, 1969: 10-11). Tocqueville (1969: 555-558; 1968b: 200) acknowledges powerful countertrends threatening equality. Though inclusive, his generalization is historically restricted. It does not identify a first, absolute, primordial cause or trend. For instance, Christianity long antedates and is an important source of modern equality. In asserting that the democratic revolution will elude the efforts of people to resist it, his (1969: 11-12) prediction seems to postulate a force controlling people regardless of their will; but Tocqueville only means to conclude that, under what analysis identifies as probable future conditions, people are likely to act in predictable ways. Within the parameters established by this trend toward equality they will make the decisive choices determining what will be combined with equality. However deterministic Tocqueville's prediction may appear, taken in context it is consistent with his understanding of the place of prediction in social science.

The abstraction necessary in the search for social scientific truth reflects the limits of human intelligence (1969: 437-438). Individuals cannot perceive all the ways in which they both resemble and differ from one another. The attempt to do so produces a wilderness of blinding detail, making vision impossible; hence they resort to abstraction. People identify similarities and then state general ideas and generalizations presupposing the validity of these abstractions. The resulting general ideas are necessarily distorting because no two beings are exactly alike and no laws "can be applied indiscriminately in the same way to several objects at once" (1969: 437). Though indispensable, general ideas are limited in that "what is gained in extent is always lost in exactitude."

The conclusion to Volume 1 of *Democracy* gives a more positive account of abstraction. Having treated the destiny of the United States in detail, Tocqueville (1969: 408) proposes from one viewpoint to clarify its overall shape. Like a traveler leaving a city and climbing an overlooking hill, the details will be obscured but its basic shape will be clarified. Tocqueville's imagery stresses the loss of valuable detail less than the gain in clarity and comprehensiveness resulting from the larger view.

The historian (or social scientist) must pursue social scientific truth even while recognizing its limitations. Individuals must attend carefully to the facts. In testing ideas the facts must be honestly represented as they are seen (1955: xii), never consciously fitted "to opinions instead of subjecting opinions to the facts" (1969: 19; see also p. 20; 1968b: 268). Recognizing that the facts do not speak for themselves—"nothing is so hard to appreciate as facts" (1969: 214)—one must, like Tocqueville (1862, 2: 207), seek to derive from them their general truths. One must also be willing to engage in the "slow, detailed, and conscientious" intellectual efforts that increase knowledge, avoiding quickly formulated generalizations that produce only superficial and uncertain results (1969: 440). Sometimes more than a year's research was spent on one short chapter in *The Old Regime* (1955: xv), and Volumes 1 and 2 of *Democracy* did not appear until three and eight years, respectively, after Tocqueville's return to France from America. Recognizing the distinction between them, social scientists must penetrate surface appearances to ascertain underlying realities. They must recognize that science cannot determine our values, which instead are derived from other sources. Historians must base their work on the appreciation of authentic human values and orient it toward promoting them. They must recognize that their values produce a selective focus so that, far from completely apprehending reality, they see it from one viewpoint only. Historians must use abstractions and seek to establish generalizations while recognizing the limitations of both. They must give appropriate weight to the general, particular, chance, and accidental factors in history and recognize the inexplicability of some events. They must avoid the temptation to overemphasize the importance of one or a few general causes. Even more, they must avoid using a few such causes to construct absolute, deterministic systems which, in asserting that the course of history is determined by blind causes that people are powerless to influence by acts of will and moral choice, encourage the passivity that reduces rather than promotes freedom. Tocqueville's historian faces a difficult task.

COMPARATIVE-HISTORICAL METHOD

Historical Method

We distinguish two aspects of the comparative-historical approach to which Tocqueville's name is linked: the historical or genetic method and the comparative method. The former assumes that we understand phenomena by explaining how they have come to be what they are; that is, by analyzing their development and evolution. Asked by Senior about equality, Tocqueville (Tocqueville and Senior, 1872, 1: 93) replied that "to explain it, I must begin historically." While preparing to write *The Old Regime* Tocqueville (1862, 2: 241-242), expressed his desire to improve on existing accounts of the French Revolution and contemporary France by overcoming the chief deficiency of their authors, namely, inadequate understanding of the preceding historical periods. Similarly, the conclusion to *The Old Regime* (1955: 210) asserts that to understand the French Revolution and postrevolutionary France requires understanding of the old regime. In general, "I should find it impossibly difficult to explain what now exists without saying how I understand what went before" (1969: 738).

Democracy (1969: 31-32) likens human to national development. To understand the adult requires knowledge of the child's first impressions. "The whole man is there . . . in the cradle." Similarly, peoples are products of their origins. The American "point of departure" is the germ of her historical development (1969: 32), making *Democracy's* chapter (1969: 31-49) on America's origins the key to the whole book.

Normally, historical origins are lost in the past. As new societies, colonies such as America provide unusually clear demonstrations of the influence of origins. Tocqueville (1969: 279) saw America's destiny in her first Puritan.

He felt that analysis of the development of European colonies furthered understanding of European society. Settlers carry with them some but not all of the heritage of their homeland. Taking root in virgin territory, the transplanted tendencies are seeds that develop according to their immanent tendencies, unencumbered by interaction with the elements with which they compete in the mother country. Study of these transplanted elements helps the analyst to understand them and ascertain their effects, effects present in the Old and New World settings alike. Somehow America's original English settlers separated the principle of equality from all the other elements in their English heritage and transported that principle alone to the New World (1969: 18); America exemplifies its free, unrestricted growth. In Canada transplanted French centralization was free to grow unencumbered by entrenched nobility; the Church; feudal, municipal, and provincial institutions; and other obstacles that impeded its growth in France. Consequently, Canada presents a particularly clear picture of the nature and defects of centralization (1955: 253-254).

Tocqueville's practice was consistent with his prescription. The first Anglo-Americans were a product of their English heritage. Tocqueville wrote extensively on England (Drescher, 1964a), and his posthumous *Journeys to England and Ireland* begins with "Reflections on English History" (1968a: 1-23). Tocqueville carries his explanation of American democracy (and English liberty) back to the decentralization and freedom of feudal England. Feudal Europe is the historical starting point of *The Old Regime* (1955, for example, pp. 14-19). Characteristically, Tocqueville's work on the American penitentiary system (coauthored with Beaumont) opens with a historical outline (Beaumont and

Tocqueville, 1964: 37-52). The historical dimension pervades the writings of this Frenchman (1955: 156) who devoted much of his life to studying history.

Comparative Approach

The other part of Tocqueville's comparative-historical method was the use of comparisons, which are essential because "the mind can gain clarity only through comparison" (quoted in Richter, 1969: 136). Though seldom mentioning France, he did not write a page of *Democracy* without thinking about his native land (1862, 1: 342): "This perpetual silent reference to France was a principle cause of the book's success." Lacking a point of comparison, he (1969: 309) professes himself able only to hazard opinions. The future remains cloudy because Christian lands are more nearly equal now than ever before in history so that "terms of comparison are lacking" (1969: 12).

Tocqueville often poses his analyses in comparative terms. *The Old Regime* (1955: x, 21) sought to explain why the Great (European) Revolution, stirrings of which were widespread throughout Europe, broke out in France and not elsewhere and why it took a different shape there. Analogous to the title of his study with Beaumont (1964), *On the Penitentiary System in the United States and Its Application in France,* his classic work (1969) on America could have been titled *On Democracy in America and Its Application in France.*

Employing what his friend Mill (1884) called the method of "concomitant variation," Tocqueville tested for cause-and-effect relationships by determining whether variation in one variable, presumed to be an independent variable or cause, was systematically linked to and followed by concomitant variation in another variable, hypothesized to be an effect. This method requires identification of variation followed by the test for concomitance. The test is achieved comparatively by determining the degree of concomitance between hypothesized cause and effect.

Concomitance between two variables establishes a strong presumption of a cause-and-effect relationship. Normally, the question of which is cause and which is effect is resolved by demonstrating that prior variation in one is followed by subsequent variation in the other. Tocqueville knew that this temporal ordering was not always apparent, making it easy to mistake cause for effect. Trade and industry have been cited as causes of the inordinate taste for physical pleasures displayed by industrialists and merchants. However, Tocqueville (1969: 552n) argues, it is this taste that induces people to pursue trade and industry where economic success enables them to appease their materialism.

Tocqueville's comparisons employed different units of analysis. Often he compared two or three nations, focusing particularly on France, England, and America. Having found important parallels in Germany, France, and England, Tocqueville (1955: 15) states the rationale for his comparative approach: "Each of the three nations helped me to a better understanding of the other two." Indeed, it is hard to think of another social scientist who so systematically compared two and three nations. Tocqueville's comparisons also included other European nations (for example, Switzerland), European colonies in North and South America (for example, Canada and Mexico), Russia, non-European nations (for example, India), as well as classic societies (for example, Rome). Other comparisons were intranational. He (1955: 212-221) compared *pays d'états* in France, especially Languedoc, with other regions to show that the greater their local independence, the more they displayed energy, initiative, prosperity, and community. He (1969) also compared the North, South, and West in the United States.

Sometimes Tocqueville employed mutually supplementary inter- and intranational comparisons. *The Old Regime* compares peasants in (1) France with those elsewhere in Europe, particularly in Germany (1955: 22-32); (2) different regions of France (1955: 175); and (3) different regions in Germany (1955: 25). Each comparison buttresses his argument that peasants were most revolutionary where their situation had improved the most in terms of liberation from feudalism.

Concerned not only with establishing but also with rejecting explanations, Tocqueville (1969: 742-744) compares New York State and Switzerland to show that democratic governments can successfully combat their natural vices, namely, hasty, tyrannical government (1969: 742). Consequently, contrary to Cherbuliez's argument, these defects are not inherent in democracy but instead are only the consequences of particular aspects of Swiss democratic government.

Tocqueville stops short of denying that race explains any variation in social behavior. During his trip to America he (1971: 392) considered whether, as held by some philosophers, human nature is the same everywhere. Given the great variation a given people may display, the analyst must be cautious in appealing to differences in human nature to explain the variation among peoples, yet there are constants that distinguish one group from another. The way Tocqueville poses the issue suggests the (possible) importance of race. Amid vast social variation, a constant effect—a people's basic character, something unchanging— remains. This constancy is presumably caused by something other than the social variation that surrounds it and despite which it manifests itself. Racial differences in human nature seems a plausible explanation of the constancy.

More typically, rather than asserting, Tocqueville either limits or denies the influence of race. Consistent with his practice of appealing to multiple as opposed to single causes, he qualifies the importance of race by citing it as one of a number of causes. For instance, he (1971: 230-231) identifies five causes that explain why American morals are the world's most chaste: (1) the physical (racial) constitution of Americans; (2) religion; (3) settled habits; (4) early marriage; and (5) the rational education of women. Sometimes, Tocqueville acknowledged the importance of race or education. Writing to Beaumont about Gobineau's *Essai sur l'inégalité des races humaines (Essay on the inequality of human races)*, Tocqueville (1862, 2: 237) gives his reaction:

> [Gobineau] has just sent me a thick book . . . in which he endeavors to prove that all that takes place in the world may be explained by the differences of race. I do not believe a word of it, and yet I think that there is in every nation, whether in consequence of race or of an education which has lasted for centuries, some peculiarity, tenacious if not permanent, which combines with all the events that befall it, and is seen both in good and in bad fortune, in every period of its history.

In another letter (1862, 2: 401), he refers to a race "inferior by nature or by education." However, difference in level of civilization does not demonstrate inherent difference in intelligence. Though less civilized, Amerindians have "displayed as much natural genius as the European peoples" (Tocqueville, 1969: 333).

Democracy (1969: 566-567) reflects his assessment of the relative importance of biological and social factors in explaining variation in human behavior and institutions. Observing that many people attribute the reserved demeanor of the English to their race, Tocqueville concludes that if this is a factor, social conditions are much more important. Tocqueville (1862, 2: 36; see also Tocqueville and Beaumont, 1968: 159) writes a friend that he never admits the importance of racial differences "except as a last resource, and when I have nothing else to say." His preference is always to seek a social explanation.

Tocqueville offers a telling account both of the appeal of racial explanations and of their scientific shortcomings. Though race undoubtedly influences human behavior and institutions, it is impossible to specify the extent of that influence. "So we can at will either infinitely restrict its action or extend it to things according to the needs of the discourse" (quoted in Schleifer, 1980: 68).

Confronting theories asserting the preponderant importance of race as a cause in history and society, Tocqueville rejects them as he does all deterministic explanations of human behavior. In a letter about *Lec-*

tures on the History of France to its author, Sir James Stephen, Tocqueville (1862, 2: 399) notes that he must disagree with that part of the work that attaches "such decisive importance to race" and that attributes "the freedom of the English principally to their Teutonic blood." Tocqueville's (1980: 320-322) best-known rejection of racial explanations occurs in his correspondence with Gobineau (Tocqueville, 1968b: 188-336). As a preliminary consideration he notes the difficulty of classifying people into racial groups except where clear, externally recognizable differences such as color exist. When, however, racial explanations are applied within one of the great racial groups, for example, the white race, then reasoning becomes lost in a web of uncertainty because "when, how, and in what proportions the mixing took place which produced men who now show no visible trace of their origin" is lost in the past (1980: 321). Even apart from this often insurmountable difficulty, innumerable comparisons show how much groups vary. Julius Caesar must have thought that British savages were destined to vegetate in a remote corner of the world that the Romans were by nature destined to rule. Amerindians (1969: 29, 318) were once a proud, energetic, independent race; many remain so, but others have been enervated by their contact with European settlers. The English aristocracy gives England one of the best and Ireland one of the world's worst governments (1968a: 151-152). The English differ depending on whether they live in England or America and, in America, on whether they live on the northern (Ohio) or southern (Kentucky) banks of the Ohio River. The French in Languedoc (1955: 212-221) showed far more of the virtues Tocqueville valued—independence and public spirit—than did those living elsewhere in France. In sum, far from there being sufficient concomitance between race and its presumed effects to validate racial explanations of society and history, the lack of such concomitance requires us to reject such explanations.

Tocqueville, then, feels that race may account for some variation in human behavior. In their less extreme versions he has no moral objection to racial explanations and feels they might be consistent with the relevant evidence; but, having both moral and scientific grounds to do so, he (1968b: 231) rejects "extreme applications" of racial explanations of society and history. According to Tocqueville, such materialistic, deterministic, fatalistic, and immoral doctrines degrade people by denying their freedom and reducing rather than promoting their propensity to exercise it. Tocqueville (1968b: 308) found Gobineau's racial doctrine, which asserted not only the inferiority and superiority of different races but the inevitable decline of all races, including the Anglo-Saxon, so repugnant that after years of exchanging letters about race, letters that reveal how greatly Gobineau's racial doctrines distressed him,

Tocqueville finally wrote Gobineau to say that he no longer wished to discuss his racial doctrines with him.

At its simplest, the method of concomitant variation identifies one cause of one effect. Typically, however, there are complications. Tocqueville postulates no one-to-one relationship between cause and effect. A single cause may have multiple effects just as a single effect may have multiple causes. Thus a hypothesized "cause" might be a single cause or an interrelated complex of causes; similarly, the effect might be an effect or a complex of effects. Tocqueville (see, for example, 1969: 645-651, especially p. 647; 1862, 1: 311) demonstrates how different, even opposite effects, may result from the same cause. He also analyzes reciprocal influences between and among variables; vis-à-vis each other, two variables may simultaneously be both cause and effect.

Causes vary in strength and explanations are competitive. Often the explanatory task is to assess the relative importance of different causes that may be hypothesized to be mutually complementary or that competing theories identify as decisive. Concerned with the originality of his explanations, Tocqueville often pits the explanatory power of a variable in a competing explanation against that of one in his explanation. In the example analyzed below, Tocqueville seeks to establish the relative importance of three variables.

The equally favorable physical environments of North and South America have not produced comparable results. In contrast to the peace, prosperity, happiness, and freedom, in the United States, "there are no nations on earth more miserable than those of South America" (1969: 306). Moreover, though its richly endowed virgin territory is far more favorable to prosperity than Europe's, South America, quite in contrast to the United States, has not even been able to attain the level of European society. Tocqueville (1969: 306; see also p. 305, 308) concludes that "physical causes do not influence the destiny of nations as much as is supposed."

If physical causes are not decisive, perhaps the laws are. Though acknowledging them to be of greater importance than physical circumstances, Tocqueville (1969: 307) denies their decisiveness. With as favorable a physical environment as the United States, Mexico has also adopted the essential aspects of her legal structure (her federal laws) but cannot succeed at democratic government. Tocqueville concludes that it must be something other than physical environment or law that explains the rule of free, prosperous democracy in the United States.

Tocqueville uses both inter- and intranational comparisons to demonstrate the decisive importance of mores. In sparsely settled New England people left comfortable circumstances to seek their fortunes in the wilderness. Though forced to pay a much higher price for their more heavily populated land, French Canadians were less willing to become pioneers. If in the American West society seems to rule by chance and public affairs are conducted in a disorderly, feverish manner, in the East government is strong, orderly, and mature. Americans share a common origin, language and religion making "all arguments derived from the nature of the country and differences of laws" irrelevant (1969: 307). What differentiates New Englanders from French Canadians, and American Easterners from Westerners, is their mores.

Tocqueville uses the preceding examples to deny the decisive importance of given variables (physical circumstances, laws) by showing a lack of concomitance between them and the variation in question and to assert the importance of a third variable (mores) by demonstrating its concomitance with that variation. Where causes produce the same effect it is difficult to distinguish their separate contributions and hence to determine their relative importance. In contrast, where causes have opposite effects their relative importance is more easily assessed. To seal his argument Tocqueville pits mores against laws and physical environment. Doing so enables him to demonstrate not only their power vis-à-vis each of the other two variables taken separately but even against their combined power. He identifies two contrasting configurations demonstrating the importance of mores: Favorable mores will overcome unfavorable laws and physical circumstances; favorable circumstances and laws, however, will not overcome unfavorable mores. In stating this conclusion Tocqueville does not cite supporting empirical illustrations. Mexico illustrates the case of favorable circumstances and laws but unfavorable mores. However, his argument includes no instance illustrating the contrary combination. The immediate focus of his analysis, the United States, is favorable on all three accounts, which helps to explain why Tocqueville uses international comparisons to assess the relative importance of his three variables. Nonetheless, even though he does not offer an empirical illustration of each of his theoretical configurations, the logic of his analysis is clear.

Tocqueville demonstrates repeatedly the necessity of analyzing phenomena in context. English elites, accustomed to working together and sharing an interest in perpetuating the established order, defended the established faith from attack (1955: 153-154). When men of letters in France attacked the church other elites not only failed to defend it, but helped spread irreligion among the people (1955: 148-155). In short, outwardly similar groups may respond differently to the same stimulus; alternatively, the same cause may produce different effects. *The Old Regime* (1955: 88-89) also illustrates how outwardly similar phenomena may be fundamentally different in nature, result from different causes, and have different effects. Burke feels that the ease with which French commoners could secure a nobility-conferring post was analogous to the open English aristocracy. Tocqueville rejects the analogy. First, the boundaries of the two aristocracies were different. In France those boundaries were sharp but relatively easily crossed; in England the boundaries were hazy but therefore not easily traversed. Second, mobility resulted from different causes. French kings distributed titles lavishly, first to lower the prestige of the nobility, later to raise money. Though Tocqueville does not address the point explicitly, in England mobility into the aristocracy was presumably controlled largely by the English aristocracy itself. Finally, the effects of mobility were different. Those who entered the French nobility were shunned by the older nobility as upstarts. Furthermore, the high rates of mobility increased the envy among those left behind, increasing personal and class antagonisms. England's vague boundaries encouraged the illusion by those on the outskirts that they were, indeed, a part of the nobility, which encouraged them to identify and cooperate with it. Not only did mobility mean crossing a different kind of line, but it resulted from different causes and produced different effects. Surface similarity may simply mask underlying differences.

This sensitivity to contexts and the resulting suspicion of historical analogies pervades Tocqueville's work. "Nothing is more deceitful than historical resemblances" (1862, 2: 384). He rejects comparisons of contemporary France with Augustinian Rome, (1862, 2: 384) as well as many popular French-English comparisons. Though he acknowledges "some resemblance in the two Revolutions, and though Louis Philippe seemed to be the ghost of William the Third," he feels that the analogy between the English (Glorious) Revolution of 1688 and the French Revolution of 1830 was more misleading than instructive. In *Recollections* (1970: 64) he argues that the anxiety of English and French Kings to avoid the mistakes of their predecessors resulted in disastrous policies. Historical analogies deceive the hasty historian just as they lead kings astray.

Two Logics of Control

Tocqueville uses two different logics of control. At times he controls as much as possible in order to isolate the effect of a single variable. For instance, he (1969: 565-567; see also Beaumont and Tocqueville, 1964: 91ff.) seeks to demonstrate the impact of equality on social intercourse. Their heritage makes American settlers similar to the English, the chief difference being that whereas America is egalitarian, in England an aristocracy of money has succeeded one of birth. This single decisive difference in the midst of vast similarity facilitates analysis of the consequences of inequality versus equality: In contrast to Americans who, meeting as strangers, assume their equality and mix easily, English strangers, concerned about but unable to judge their relative status, prudently avoid contact. More generally, Americans are frank and open and the English are more reserved. Tocqueville uses the same logic in intranational comparisons, which control even more variation. His American East-West comparison controls many possible differences rendering arguments appealing to those differences "irrelevant" (1969: 307). Again, the similarities among Americans permit Tocqueville to account for differences among people living in the North, South, and West as follows: The North is an older, more mature, settled region, the West is young and immature, and the South has slavery.

The same logic applies to developmental comparisons. European nations initially had the same institutions (1955: 14). From this common point of departure England and France increasingly diverged. Establishing their initial similarity helps Tocqueville (1955: 98) pinpoint a crucial cause of their initial and subsequent divergence: different taxation policies. In England the principle of "No taxation without the people's consent" remained in effect, and the rich were subjected to heavier taxes than the poor. In France the king exceeded his tax levying authority, and it was the poor who were taxed most heavily.

Elsewhere the success of Tocqueville's argument depends, not on establishing similarity but, if anything, on variation in context. The greater the variability of the contexts in which its hypothesized theoretical relationships hold, the more widely applicable a theory is. Tocqueville showed that this theory applied in Old and New World contexts, to both premodern and modern societies, to aristocratic and democratic societies, to agrarian and industrializing societies, to old and new societies, and to societies with different cultures (for example, French versus English). Though Tocqueville died before the full flowering of the Industrial Revolution, clearly he felt his theory would apply to industrialized societies. Contemporary applications of his theory beyond the contexts in which Tocqueville applied them, for example, to the developing nations of today (see, for example, Huntington, 1968) or to postindustrial society are consistent with his understanding of his theory. And though Tocqueville focused on societies, there is no reason not to apply it to less inclusive structures such as organizations (see, for example, Lipset et al., 1956).

Historical and Comparative Analysis
in Tocqueville

Though analytically distinct, in Tocqueville the historical and comparative approaches are supplementary, where they are not fused. Tocqueville is forever comparing nations, analyzing historical development, and comparing development in one country with that in another. Like comparisons between units, longitudinal comparisons may be used to establish variation, which is one reason Tocqueville employs the historical method. The use of historical variation to establish concomitance is central to *The Old Regime*. Analyzing French society over centuries enables Tocqueville to demonstrate how the gradual increase in centralization was linked to the gradual reduction in community, freedom, and authority.

Tocqueville's (1955: 253-254) comparison of Canada and the United States combines historical and comparative analysis. Because centralized administration in Canada and decentralized administration in the United States both grew unencumbered, comparing the two countries provides an unusually clear picture of their contrasting effects.

As employed by Tocqueville the historical method helps analysts to: treat phenomena and their contexts in depth; take into account the individuality of the phenomena and historical contexts they seek to explain; minimize any tendency to equate phenomena merely on the basis of outward similarities; retain awareness that in different contexts outwardly and even basically similar phenomena may have different causes and effects; and help control variables interacting with the causes and effects they seek to establish. A disadvantage of the historical approach is the one-case/many-variables problem as well as the inherent difficulty of generalizing from one instance. Comparisons help overcome the dangers of the latter. They provide additional opportunities to control variables interacting with the causes and effects of which the analyst seeks to establish. The disadvantage of such comparisons is that, being more abstract, they may destroy the very individuality of the phenomena and historical contexts that the analyst seeks to capture. Comparisons may also encourage equating phenomena on the basis of outward similarities and thereby produce insensitivity to the way in which in different contexts seemingly similar phenomena may not only be the product of different causes but may have different effects.

Tocqueville adjusted his approach to his explanatory goal. Sometimes he focused on explaining a particular historical event, for example, the French Revolution, other times on developing and applying a theory, for example, his theory of freedom (1969). Often he (1955) was concerned with both. Combining historical and comparative analysis, he used the strengths of each to compensate for the weaknesses of the other.

A TOCQUEVILLIAN PERSPECTIVE

Tocqueville offers varying evaluations of people and their motivations. In a pessimistic moment he (1862, 2: 51) wonders if opinions and feelings are not merely cloaks for the only human motive, selfishness. A more balanced assessment holds that "neither very good nor very bad," humans are a "strange combination . . . of good and evil, of grandeur and baseness" (1862, 1: 392; see also p. 327). In rare moments, as in the French Revolution, people rise to heights of heroic virtue and grandeur that provide lasting inspiration for future generations. Tocqueville (1862, 1: 300, see also 1968b: 324-325) himself loved "mankind in general" even though "I constantly meet with individuals whose baseness revolts me."

Interests, Ideas, and Passions

Tocqueville (1969: 373; see also p. 167) distinguishes between material interests and "opinions and feelings, which may be called man's immaterial interests." Interest overlaps with ideas and passions (feelings). Ideas define interests. It is in terms of cognitions and definitions that potential ends, both material and immaterial, are defined as interests and ranked in terms of their relative importance. Ideas encourage people to be materialistic or spiritualistic, egoistic or altruistic, and define choices as either moral or immoral. In the modern world the demand for equality and in free societies the demand for independence are reigning interests (1969: 176). These interests are defined by people's ideas about what equality and freedom mean in all their social, political, economic, and other dimensions.

But, equally, interests influence ideas. Southerners justify black agricultural slave labor by asserting that blacks can labor in the South without danger in contrast to whites for whom such labor in that region is fatal (1969: 352; see also 1968b: 305-306). Even religious ideas, which do so much to define ideal interests, accommodate to the interest situations of their adherents. The varying interests of different societies and, within given societies, of their constituent groups, has given rise to variation in Christian teachings (1968b: 205; 1969: 466-467). In America Christianity defines interests so that people may simultaneously and with equal fervor pursue their material and their religiously defined ideal interests (1969: 47, 448-499, 528-530).

Given his concern with freedom and morality and his conception of people as moral beings, Tocqueville is particularly concerned with the relationship between material and ideal interests, a relationship itself mediated by ideas. Preferring to believe they are doing the right thing, people develop ideas that justify the pursuit of their interests. All humankind develops moral codes reflecting the universal needs and interests of social life itself, turning necessities into virtues. Different nations, classes, and castes develop codes of honor reflecting their distinctive needs, interests, and characteristic behaviors, again turning necessities into virtues (1969: 617-627). The Romans valued courage, even equating it with virtue; the European feudal nobility, military courage and loyalty; and democratic Americans bold, industrious pursuit of money. Such justifications shade off into the use of ideas to cloak underlying interests, which in extreme cases becomes hypocrisy (1970: 110).

None of this means that ideas or the ideal interests they define are merely rationalizations or justifications of, or mere emanations from, underlying material interests that alone are real. Ideas and ideal interests develop to some degree according to their own dynamic, are partially independent of material interests, and are just as real and important. Religious ideas define many ideal interests, for example, the nature of immortality and happiness in the hereafter. People have ideal interests in being moral as defined by their religious and other ideas. In defining moral codes ideas define the ideal interests that people seek to realize even as they pursue material and other interests. In some cases ideal interests are of such overriding importance that people will sacrifice everything, including material interests and life itself, in pursuit of them. Muslim warriors fought to the death in holy wars; and the founders of New England sacrificed friends, families, and country for their religious convictions (1969: 47). Once born even those moral and honor codes originating in largely materialistic needs become invested with a life of their own. They may outlive the interests that originally gave rise to them and conflict with new group interests. Even at the expense of their economic and political interests, impoverished and politically weak aristocrats may disdain bourgeoisie money-making pursuits or marriage with daughters of the prosperous bourgeoisie. In sum, ideas and interests, as well as ideal and material interests, stand in a relationship of partial autonomy coupled with mutual influence.

People have an interest in expressing and satisfying their feelings. They may also become passionately attached to their ideas (see, for example, 1969: 176) or to material possibilities, turning each into interests. Indeed, it is this affective attachment that largely defines a material goal or an idea and its implications for action as an interest. Strong emotions constitute and also help to create and define interests, but the influence between them and other interests is reciprocal. Self-interest creates its own feelings (1968b: 172), and deep emotions are normally aroused only when material interests are threatened (1969: 183). Just as interests do, so also do ideas strongly influence, strengthen, and create feelings and emotions. Normally, people remain relatively passive so long as their personal feelings are not aroused (1968b: 172). Even when intense, these feelings usually do not propel people very far or high unless they are reinforced and justified by ideas. "Add to passions born of self-interest the aim to change the face of the world and to regenerate the human race: only then will you see what men are really capable of. That is the history of the French Revolution" (1968b: 172). In an earlier work, *The Old Regime*, Tocqueville (1955: 138-169, especially p. 142) shows how the philosopher's ideas cloaked, canalized, justified, reinforced, and, indeed, created many of the interests and passions causing the French Revolution. Socialist philosophy kindled the passions and class warfare that erupted into the 1848 February Revolution in France (1970: 74-76; see also p. 165). In contrast to America where "personalities are everything, principles insignificant . . . in France, and elsewhere in Europe, society is divided by two or three great ideas around which positive interests and passions rally" (quoted in Pierson, 1938: 535-536). Ideas, interests, and emotions overlap conceptually, empirically interpenetrate, and mutually influence one another.

Their mutual influence explains why the different types of interest are often congruent. At the same time, given that they follow partially independent paths, their relations may vary from congruence to independence (making it possible for one to be hurt while another is not) to conflict. Passions may be wounded though material interests are not (1969: 383). In France's old regime the enduring passion for the ideal interest in equality conflicted with the behavior of the French, motivated by their material interests as defined by the existing social structure.

Though Tocqueville distinguishes three main types of interest, his analyses frequently employ the concept of interest without further specification (for example, 1836: 87). Elsewhere, in asserting the importance of one or two kinds without mentioning the remainder he seems to imply that what has been identified is basic. Nonetheless, what is most characteristic of his work is his emphasis on the importance of all three and their mutual and, particularly preceding and during periods of major social change, changing relations. For example, *The Old Regime* analyzes the causes and consequences of the French literati's addiction to ideas (1955: 138-169); the impact of the people's two ruling passions (hatred of inequality and desire for freedom; 1955: 207); the peasants' obsessive passion for land ownership (1955: 24); the middle class's equally obsessive passion for office (1955: 91); the peasants' ruling interests and emotions (1955: 31); France's increasing (group) individualism (1955: 96); and the revolutionary tension created by the government's simultaneous encouragement and thwarting of materialistic interests (1955: 179). Similarly, different passages in *Democracy* explain human behavior and group relations in terms of one kind of interest, two, or all three kinds.

The interests of individuals and groups exist in a complex array of congruence and conflict. Furthermore, dominant interests vary from age to age, group to group, individual to individual. Tocqueville postulates no universal primary motivation, whether that be the desire for power, esteem, glory, material goods, immortality, or whatever. However, in all ages there is "some peculiar and predominating element which controls all the rest" and which "almost always engenders some seminal thought or ruling passion which in the end drags all other feelings and ideas along in its course" (1969: 504). Equality reigns as the dominant element in the modern age.

The particular interest of the moment prevails in all people (1969: 264). Usually such interests are those private interests that motivate most behavior (1969: 512). The small, recurrent, everyday interest is decisive. Collectively they are the source of the "great interest we take in life" (1836: 78). Local interests normally engage people more than do general national interests (1969: 162; see also 1955: 51, 202). Only under unusual but important conditions of national crises or social change are people motivated not by routine everyday interests but by national interests or those newly shaped by abstract ideas.

Given the importance of immediate, personal, recurrent interests, the importance to individuals of many phenomena is proportional to their place in their everyday lives. Most of life is lived locally in mundane, everyday social, economic, and political contexts and is oriented toward and most affected by what occurs there. Even events with national dimensions such as war and economic cycles of prosperity and depression become most relevant as they affect and are mediated in terms of the individual's everyday world. The everyday world's ideas, passions, and ideal and material interests, and their associated habits carry over into and influence the individual's orientation toward and behavior within the noneveryday world. Accordingly, Tocqueville's analyses often build from the bottom up, analyzing everyday life and then tracing its embodiment in and impact on supralocal institutions. *Democracy*

(1969: 61-170) first treats the township, next state government, and only then the federal government and the Constitution. The Foreword to *The Old Regime* (1955: vii-xv) makes clear Tocqueville's intent to seek the passions, ideas, and interests basic to the French in their personal lives, and the book treats increasing centralization largely in terms of how it affected all classes in their everyday lives. Of course, ever sensitive to reciprocal effects, Tocqueville also assesses the impact of supralocal institutions on everyday life.

Where the habits, passions, interests, and ideas of people, particularly in their everyday lives, are favorable to it, Tocqueville predicts freedom in the longer run even if formal legal structures, national political institutions, and the national government all oppose it. On the other hand, where these same factors oppose freedom Tocqueville held but little hope unless, of course, national structures could be altered to produce a favorable effect on everyday life. Specifically, decentralization promotes freedom.

Personal interest is "the only stable point in the human heart" (1969: 239) and material interests are "more visible, tangible, and permanent than opinions" (1969: 187). Ideas and passions are sometimes stable, sometimes not. Relative to material interests, however, they are unstable. Tocqueville's analyses of revolutionary society and the modern world are concerned with the instability of the ideas and passions of the multitudes as constant threats to the order without which freedom cannot survive.

Basic Causes

Seeking to explain various phenomena and different kinds of variation, Tocqueville appeals to different causal factors. He (1968b: 212, 267-268) feels Mohammedanism was responsible for the stagnation and decadence of Islamic countries. The combination of slavery and English character "explains the mores and social condition of the [American] South" (1969: 35). Explaining Amerindian resistance to Western civilization, Tocqueville (1969: 327) notes that once a people have become accustomed to hunting as a way of life, they disdain settling down and the drudgery of agriculture. *The Old Regime* (1955: 98-99) maintains that, given the existing balance of forces, what could otherwise have been just another event in the ebb and flow of power, the king's arbitrary imposition of a new tax, was sufficient to nudge France off the road of freedom onto that of tyranny and revolution. Rejecting Gobineau's racial explanations, Tocqueville (1968b: 228) suggests following instead the traditional practice of seeing "the cause of human events in the influence of certain men, of certain emotions, of certain thoughts, and of certain beliefs."

He often asserts the power of society vis-à-vis even its most powerful members. The state of society was generally more powerful than the French kings themselves, but Tocqueville (1969: 641) also recognizes the influence of the great leader. World history suggests that "it is less the force of an argument than the authority of a name which has brought about great and rapid changes in accepted ideas." A French monarch of the caliber of Frederick the Great might have been able to redirect the French Revolution and preserve the monarchy (1955: 165; see also p. 209). His unfinished sequel (1968b: 31, 142-146) to *The Old Regime* intended to analyze the interplay between that extraordinary genius, Napoleon, and the times.

Tocqueville (1969: 51-54, 456) identifies laws of inheritance as an important influence and as an indicator (1969: 722) of a society's position on the aristocracy-democracy continuum. Laws that keep a family's inheritance intact by transmitting it to a single heir perpetuate inequality in contrast to those that, dividing it among heirs, promote equality. Primogeniture was crucial to an aristocracy whose power was based on control of the land. By maintaining the land intact from generation to generation primogeniture perpetuated the power of individual families and ultimately the aristocracy itself. "Whenever there is a great change in human institutions, one always finds that one of the causes is the laws of inheritance" (1969: 349).

The formal legal structure of government is also important. Democratic nations face the problem of ensuring that the people have sufficient but not excessive control over their elected officials. Tocqueville feels that (1862, 2: 30) "the fate of the modern world depends on its solution." Yet he (1969: 744; 1966: 768-769; 1862, 2: 230) repeatedly holds that laws, constitutions, and the formal structure of government are less important than widely believed. "Political laws are no more than the expression of" a society's social state (1969: 51) and the social condition provides the decisive context affecting such institutions and their consequences. Because they are one factor that can easily be changed by lawmakers, it is often regrettable that laws are not more important. If freedom were simply a matter of ratifying the right constitution and of passing the right laws, establishing it would be far easier than it is (1862, 2: 230). Although he recognizes the importance of laws, Tocqueville's hopes for the efficacy of most legislative enactments are circumscribed.

Concerned to highlight the originality of his own work, in asserting the importance of a cause he (1969: 51) may note surprise that others have not recognized its importance, for example, his discussion of inheritance laws. Similarly, he often downplays the importance of causes widely held to be decisive. "Physical causes do not influence the destiny of nations as much as is supposed" (1969: 306). He also ranks causes in terms of their relative importance. Collectively these statements establish Tocqueville's hierarchy of causal importance.

Democracy (1969: 308) gives two rankings (within each ranking factors are cited in order of decreasing importance): (1) social conditions, laws, and circumstances; (2) mores, laws, and physical causes. The rankings are similar in placing laws second and circumstances or physical conditions, two overlapping phenomena, last. Ironically, the factor identified in each list as most important is missing from the other list. Perhaps that is appropriate, because each list is headed by a factor that Tocqueville asserts to be of primary importance.

Mores is an abstract, inclusive concept that Tocqueville (1969: 274, 287, 305, 308, 311-312, 341, 376) defines and uses in various ways. The concept subsumes both behavioral and cognitive dimensions. It refers not only to opinions, beliefs, and ideas but also to the manners, habits, customs, and usages that follow from and are congruent with them. Tocqueville (1969: 287; see also p. 305n; 1862, 2: 230) says that he uses the term to refer to the "whole moral and intellectual state of a people." At its core mores refers to morals, and most especially, to ideas.

Tocqueville endlessly emphasizes the primacy of mores that are more powerful than laws and institutions (1862, 2: 230). His January 1848 speech (1969: 749-758) to the French Chamber of Deputies asserts the importance of political factors. Within the political realm, not the laws, but the "spirit of the government," that is, the mores animating those in power, is crucial (1969: 758). Among mores, ideas, particularly as public opinion, are decisive. More powerful than kings (1862, 1: 390), in both America and France it reigns as the dominant power (1969: 124; see also pp. 435, 448). Public opinion caused the various French Revolutions and coups d'etat, including that of 1789 (1955: 138ff; 1968b: 101, 111; 1970: 74). "Whatever anyone says, it is ideas that stir the world and not blind needs" (1968a: 58). Feelings and ideas "are responsible for the changed state of the world" (1969: 418). Not interests but common ideas are the basis of societal integration (1969: 373). In short, "ideas, often very abstract ideas, in the end govern society" (1862, 1: 351).

Tocqueville's depth imagery orders phenomena in terms of importance. He contrasts outward, surface appearances with the deeper, underlying, hidden realities that control and animate them. Ideas lie at the core of social reality. Accordingly, ever seeking to probe as deeply as possible, Tocqueville repeatedly states his intent to penetrate the surface of institutions to the ideas, opinions, and mores that undergrid them (1970: 11-12; see also 1968b: 54), to the underlying spirit animating society and institutions (1955: 175), and to the ideas, feelings, and mores basic to the social structure (1955: viii, 1862, 1: 360).

"The importance of mores is a universal truth . . . which . . . occupies the central position in my thoughts: all my ideas come back to it in the end" (1969: 308). *Democracy,* the source of this statement, makes a similar point about the equality of conditions in America. "The more I studied American society, the more clearly I saw equality of conditions as the creative element from which each particular fact derived, and all my observations constantly returned to this nodal point" (1969; 9).[1] Tocqueville spares no pains in asserting the importance of the equality of conditions. It is a basic fact with prodigious influence on both political and civil society. "It creates opinions, gives birth to feelings [and] suggests customs" (1969: 9). Penetrating everything (1969: 56), it "modifies whatever it does not create" (1969: 9).

Indeed, Volume 1 of *Democracy* (1969: 9-20) is consistent with these assertions of equality's importance in the "Author's Introduction." *Democracy's* readers, then, may be surprised by the qualifications in the Preface to Volume 2 (1969: 417-418). Acknowledging Volume 1's emphasis on the equality of conditions, Tocqueville warns the reader against a serious misunderstanding of his work. He does not consider equality anything like a sole cause. Rather, many American mores are due to factors such as the nature of the country, the origin of the colonists, their religion, enlightenment, and former habits that are distinct from or even antithetical to it. Similarly, much of what occurs in Europe is explained by factors untouched by equality. Asserting his awareness of such powerful causes, Tocqueville (1969: 417) says that the theme of his book does not deal with them. *Democracy* was intended not "to account for all our inclinations and our ideas, but, only . . . to demonstrate how equality has modified both."

The Preface does not characterize the equality of conditions as a pervasive, dominant influence; indeed, it mentions other powerful factors and, including no assessment of relative power, makes no explicit claim about its relative importance. Rather, on the implicit assumption of its presumably considerable but still quite possibly less than decisive and, in any case, yet to be determined importance, the Preface says that *Democracy* seeks only to assess its effects. In contrast to the Preface, which merely identifies equality's influence as Tocqueville's focus, the

---

1. This passage from *Democracy* may be compared with his analysis of English society (Tocqueville, 1968a: 1-107, 79) which stresses the apparent equality coupled with the advantage conferred by wealth:

Apparent equality, real privileges of wealth, greater perhaps than in any country of the world.

Central idea; all the facts bring my attention back to it.

Introduction directs attention to equality as a ubiquitous, dominant influence (though not, therefore, the only important influence).

Ironically, though the Preface includes a far more qualified assertion about equality's influence than does the Introduction, Volume 2 presents an equally strong demonstration of its importance. Containing a comprehensive account of America, including its physical circumstances, history, federal constitution, regional differences, and three major races (Indians, blacks, and whites), Volume 1 is more empirical and more closely tied to America. The second volume is more abstract. As indicated in its contents (1969: 419-425), Volume 2 analyzes the influence of equality on intellectual life, sentiments, mores, and political society, using America as a primary example. In each instance equality's influence proves decisive. Volume 2 establishes equality's importance cumulatively, case by case, by showing its influence on an inclusive range of phenomena. In the end the reader is persuaded that in the modern world equality is indeed a fundamental fact. Notwithstanding the differences between the Introduction and the Preface, together Volumes 1 and 2 demonstrate the decisive importance of equality in both America and modern society generally.

Despite equality's pervasive influence, given differences in mores, laws, national character, and physical circumstances, equality is associated with different outcomes in different countries. Tocqueville (1969: 18) foresees the day when France will attain the almost complete equality found in America. However, he does not conclude that France will necessarily draw the same political consequences from the same social state. The American form of government is not the only one compatible with democracy. Indeed, America's and France's divergent paths to equality continue to produce divergent outcomes. Born free and egalitarian, from the beginning America enjoyed freedom's benefits (1969: 18, 432), whereas France has suffered the unhappy legacy of revolution, including individualism and mutual animosity between classes (1969: 432-433). As a result, the democratic revolution in France occurred "without those changes in laws, ideas, customs, and mores which were needed to make that revolution profitable" (1969: 13; see also 1862, 2: 384). Again exemplifying the importance of treating phenomena in their unique historical configurations, Tocqueville notes how in the American context equality is associated with freedom, in the French with tyranny.

Tocqueville's works generally assert the primacy of mores, but *Democracy* asserts the primacy of both mores and equality of conditions. Circumstances or laws, sometimes singly but generally in combination, create the social state that in turn is the prime cause of the most important laws, customs, and ideas of a nation (1969: 50). Here and elsewhere, *Democracy* (1969: 9, 18, 328, 417-418) identifies the social condition as the cause of the mores. Ever concerned with mores, Tocqueville (1969: 9, 18, 417-418) examines the social condition, for example, equality of conditions, as their primary determinant. However, he is always concerned with reciprocal influences and explained outcomes as the product of a conjunction of factors. Explaining a given social or historical phenomenon may require appeal to the social conditions or mores, or both, and quite probably additional factors as well. Where more than one factor is relevant, their reciprocal effects and the way in which the impact of a given factor varies depending on the context constituted by other relevant factors must be taken into account. The social condition, including one of its key variable aspects, inequality-equality, and mores reciprocally influence each other. Egalitarian social conditions foster demands for equality and freedom. These demands in turn helped cause the French Revolution and the transition from aristocracy to democracy in the modern world, generally. If equality has causal primacy vis-à-vis mores, Tocqueville feels that mores govern history and society directly, powerfully, and proximately. Social conditions cause mores, which themselves constitute the core of society.

THE THEORY

Variables

Freedom-Tyranny. "According to the modern, the democratic, and . . . the only just notion of liberty, every man, being presumed to have received from nature the intelligence necessary for his own general guidance, is inherently entitled to be uncontrolled by his fellows in all that only concerns himself, and to regulate at his own will his own destiny" (1836: 90). People are free to the extent that they enjoy the greatest possible room to pursue their own interests (1862, 1: 384; 836: 91). For Tocqueville freedom (liberty) is the capacity to employ morality in making choices. Whatever reduces this capacity reduces people, whatever enlarges it elevates humanity. Tocqueville (1969: 193) is concerned about all threats, external and internal, to this basic human right. People often seek to coerce each other. Tocqueville emphasized the importance of religion, morality, customs, habits, forms, laws, ideas, a free press and public opinion, openness as opposed to secrecy in government and administration, a powerful and independent judiciary, community, secondary groups and institutions, a decentralized administration, authority, the balance of power, and other factors that reduce coercion and protect individual freedom. Concerned with formal, legal, and political constraints on liberty, Tocqueville is equally concerned about informal social constraints, for example, the tyranny of the majority, and he (for example, 1969: 555-558; 1968a: 93-97) recognized the economic threat posed by the new industrial order. Though often treating freedom as freedom from external constraint, he was equally concerned about internal threats—those factors that reduce the individual's love of freedom and desire to exercise morality. He believes that in the modern world apathy, individualism, and materialism undermined people's propensity to protect and exercise their freedom. In France freedom was further undermined by exhaustion, discord, and the other legacies of revolution.

Tocqueville does not equate freedom with the absence of social control. So long as that control is voluntarily self-imposed and not forcibly imposed by some outside source, freedom is compatible with strict social control.

People and societies become "worthwhile only through their use of liberty" (1968b: 309), which is the "source of all moral greatness" (1969: 16). "The greatest of all goods" (1861, 2: 307) and an end in itself, freedom is also the indispensable source of other goods. It produces "wonders" and "marvels" (1969: 240, 244). Political freedom creates "reciprocal ties and a feeling of solidarity between all the members of a nation" (1955: 81). He (1955: xiii-xiv) recommends it as the cure for the democratic vices: mutual estrangement, preoccupation with petty personal worries, "love of gain, a fondness for business careers, the desire to get rich at all costs, [and] a craving for material comfort and easy living." Liberty would replace materialism and egoism with solidarity and concern for the public interest. Alone capable of giving "to human societies in general, and to the individuals who compose them in particular, all the prosperity and greatness of which our species is capable" (1967: 543), freedom is an integral part of a sacred complex that also includes morality, religion, order, and legal equality (1862, 1: 380; see also 1968a: 106).

Tocqueville (1968b: 166-168; 1955: 168-169) distinguishes between the love of freedom as means and end. The intellectual love of freedom derives from the benefits it bestows. People may love liberty because it eliminates the evils of despotic government or for the material rewards it confers. Others love liberty instinctively for itself, independently of material considerations. They love liberty because it enables them to live free of any restraint except the authority of God and the law; nothing could compensate them for its loss. "The man who asks of freedom anything other than itself is born to be a slave" (1955: 169). Those who love it only as a means never keep it very long. They may fail to safeguard it or, when doing so is compatible with their material interests, forgo it for despotism. Tocqueville wanted people to develop the genuine love for liberty that alone perpetuates it.

The opposite of liberty—tyranny (despotism, servitude)— exists to the degree that, being subject to coercion or restraint by others, people are not free to make moral choices.

Inequality-Equality. "An expression of envy," equality is generally "a wish that no one should be better off than oneself" (1872, 1: 92-94). Tocqueville uses the inequality-equality continuum to analyze the transition from aristocratic to democratic society. Equality includes all those ways in which people in democratic society are more equal than those in aristocratic society. The transition is a process of leveling, during which elites, losing their privileges, are reduced to the level of their former inferiors and one of inclusion and extension, whereby more and more people acquire both rights formerly enjoyed only by the privileged and new rights as well.

Though excluding inequalities common to aristocratic and democratic societies, for example, differences in rights and duties linked to age and sex, the inequality-equality continuum is inclusive. Equality means that individuals and groups are equal in terms of those attributes which would otherwise structure them hierarchically. In the following spheres equality exists to the degree that the specified conditions exist. Social: There are no hierarchical status differences, no inferiors and superiors, and no special privileges, immunities, and exemptions, only common rights. Equality does not mean that people do not form distinct groups and communities, only that such groups are not hierarchical. Economic: Differences in wages, income, property, and wealth are relatively modest. All individuals are free to compete for economic advantage. Economic advantage does not confer social or political superiority. Political: The person and the office are distinguished, with power residing in the latter. Political institutions are based on the sovereignty of the people. There is equality before the law and of voting rights. Political equality does not imply lack of political authority; it does mean that office holders are not superior to those subject to their jurisdiction and that all are free to compete for the right to exercise political power. In all three spheres—social, economic, and political— there is equality of opportunity and high rates of mobility; in none is there hereditary transmission of rank or privilege. Equality also includes mores asserting the legitimacy of equality, the illegitimacy of inequality. Egalitarian mores hold that people are basically equal, share equal rights, duties, and opportunities, and as equals have the right to be treated and regarded accordingly.

If democratic society reduces or eliminates many of the inequalities of aristocratic society, important inequalities—differences in intelligence

(1969: 56) and other natural abilities, health, luck, success, relationship to the market, material well-being, wealth, fame, esteem, and power—remain and ever generate envy in the less well-off of the better off (democratic envy). Democratic society is relatively, not absolutely, egalitarian.

Centralization-Decentralization of Administration. Tocqueville (1969: 87-89; 1966: 770-771) distinguishes between the centralization-decentralization of government and, most crucially, between the centralization-decentralization of administration. These distinctions in turn rest on that between common national interests such as defense, foreign policy, and the enactment of general laws and matters of primarily local concern such as local government, roads, schools, zoning laws, and taxes. Government is centralized when common national interests are controlled by a single center and decentralized when such control resides in different, possibly competing centers, as in extreme feudalism. Administration is centralized when matters of primarily local concern are decided nationally, and decentralized when such matters are controlled locally.[2]

Any concentration of unbalanced power destroys freedom (1969: 252). Though concerned about all such concentrations of power—for example, the informal tyranny of the majority in democratic society and an industrial aristocracy—Tocqueville felt that national governments represented the greatest potential and actual concentrations of power. The strength of any power is proportional to structural centralization (1969: 184). National governments apply power through centralized administrations the development of which they consequently encourage. These considerations underlie the importance of centralization-decentralization of administration in Tocqueville's theory.

Community-Individualism/Egoism. Structurally, community[3] exists to the degree that individuals are bound together. Social psychological community is concern for others. Egoism and individualism occur in the absence of the interaction that sustains community. Egoism is self-love. Individualism is concern for self, family, and friends. Egoism is more extreme in that, whereas individualism reduces the individual's circle of

---

2. Later *Democracy* (1969: 364-365) adds that in addition to those matters that are local versus those that are national in nature are some that are inherently mixed. They are national in that they relate to all the people in a nation but local in that they can be taken care of locally. For instance, all citizens necessarily enjoy certain civil and political rights; however, such rights need not be uniform nationally and may be regulated locally.

3. Though community can be applied to a group of any size—from the married couple to the nation-state—to distinguish it from individualism we use community to refer to groups larger than the individual's family or immediate circle of friends.

concern to a small group of family and friends, egoism reduces it to one. At their mutual boundary individualism becomes egoism. Egoism is as old as humanity itself. Of democratic origin, individualism threatens to grow proportionately with equality (1969: 506-508).

Power: Force-Authority. Power is the ability to impose one's will on the behavior or ideas of other people (adapted from Weber, 1958a: 180). Force is the threat or use of physical violence or other coercive means to compel compliance with directives. Authority is legitimate power and includes both the right to command and the duty to obey (Weber, 1968, 3: 943, 946-947). Power is legitimate to the extent that those subject to it define it as such.

Tocqueville defines some terms, for example, centralization-decentralization of administration, individualism, and egoism. However, he never offers a full definition of inequality-equality and taken individually his various, often brief, treatment of liberty remain incomplete delineations. Though central to his theory and logically implied by it as the opposite of egoism, he does not formally define "community" or other terms that he uses interchangeably with it, nor does he state systematic typologies of major variables, for example, authority. Often his meanings have to be inferred from his usage.

Theoretical Structure and Typology of Society

I derive Tocqueville's implicit typology of society by cross-classifying his two primordial variables, freedom-tyranny and inequality-equality (Figure 1).[4] These variables are continua, making the number of divisions in each arbitrary. Nevertheless, I follow Tocqueville's practice. He often characterizes societies as free or despotic and the contrast between aristocratic and democratic society is central to his analysis. He also refers to revolutionary society. Some of the names for the cells in Figure 1 are taken from Tocqueville, others are supplied.

Figure 1 defines analytic (pure) types that empirical societies only more or less closely approximate. Societies vary regionally and may have greater equality or freedom in one sphere than in another. Tocqueville called America free, yet analyzed both southern slave society and the tyranny of the majority. Societies are mixtures of different, competing, and even opposed tendencies. Though *The Old Regime* analyzes France's loss of freedom, one chapter (1955: 108-120) describes freedom

---

4. Tilton (1979: 266) uses the same procedure to derive Tocqueville's typology of society. However, the idea of doing so was suggested to me by Barclay Johnson in personal communications dating back to the early 1970s. I gratefully acknowledge my indebtedness to him.

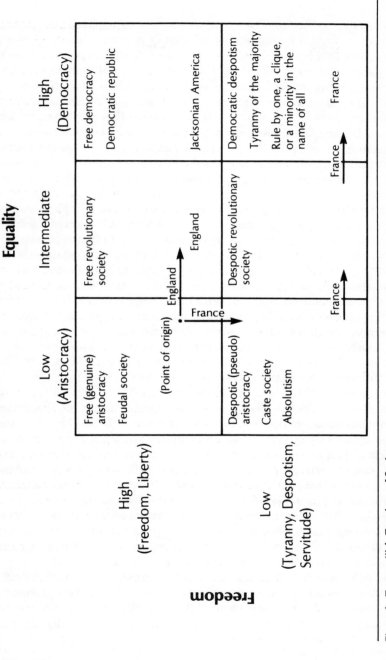

Figure 1   Tocqueville's Typology of Society

in the late old regime. Tocqueville's abstract variables are difficult to measure, further compounding difficulties in classification. Figure 1 does not reflect short-range cyclical changes. At the close of the old regime and during the beginning of the French Revolution, freedom, or at least the desire for it, burned as brightly as the passion for equality and in subsequent years periodically flamed, only to dwindle before flaming anew (1955: 208-299; see also 1968b: 126). Dichotomization ignores some linear changes that would be caught with a finer net; for instance, Tocqueville (1955: 119) feels that the trends toward centralization and loss of freedom that began in the old regime had continued—albeit momentarily reversed immediately after the outbreak of the French Revolution (1955: 208)—so that the old regime was less centralized and less despotic than the France of his own day. The placement of some societies is clearer than others. An important bastion of freedom, aristocratic England was undergoing the transition to democracy, but precisely how far she had traveled was unclear. Tocqueville (1968a: 24-107) emphasizes not only the aristocratic nature of English society but also the manifest and latent power of the democratic impulse there.

Figure 1 excludes Ireland. With the exception of relations between whites and blacks or Indians in the United States, compared to England, France, and the United States, Ireland was unique in its degree of cleavage, a cleavage produced by the superimposition of extreme class polarization on religious and national differences (1969a: 108-190; compare also Tocqueville's 1971 discussion of English-French relations in Canada). "If you want to know what can be done by the spirit of conquest and religious hatred combined with the abuses of aristocracy, but without any of its advantages, go to Ireland" (1968a: 113). Leaving the conquered Catholic Irish with many of the forms of liberty—electoral rights, freedom of the press, the right to hold meetings, *habeas corpus,* and trial by jury—the Protestant English conquerors appeared to honor liberal principles while, in fact, enjoying all the consequences of tyranny (1968a: 178, 150-151).[5] Altogether Ireland was extreme in the degree of inequality and mutual hatred between upper and lower classes that existed there. Ireland exemplified the evils of permanent inequality that Tocqueville (1968b: 229) later cites as one reason for rejecting any theory like Gobineau's that promoted them: "pride, violence, the scorn of one's fellow men, tyranny and abjection in every one of their forms."

"Aristocracy can be one of the best or one of the worst forms of government that exist in the world" (1968a: 149). Having contrasted the

---

5. In *The Old Regime* (1955: 45) and elsewhere (1968b: 155-156) Tocqueville observes that the forms of democracy can be perpetuated without its substance. In the present case he (1968a: 178) develops a different thesis. Ireland illustrates the "general truth . . . *that if the forms of liberty are allowed to subsist, sooner or later it would kill tyranny."* The Irish Catholics were beginning to use the forms of liberty they enjoyed to oppose tyranny.

English and Irish versions as prototypes of good and bad aristocracy, Tocqueville (1968a: 151) notes that they "have the same origin and manners and almost the same laws." However, embedded in different societies, one gives the English one of the world's best, the other, the Irish, one of the world's "most detestable" governments. England enjoys the benefits of aristocratic freedom while Ireland suffers the evils of extreme aristocratic tyranny.

Constructed to classify the societies on which Tocqueville concentrates, the typology in Figure 1 subsumes only a portion of either the conceptual or empirical variation. Tocqueville also discusses societies outside the Western European and American historical context, the inclusion of which would require appropriate adjustments. France was far less despotic than Russia, India, or Islamic nations. Were these and other examples included in the typology France might be classified along with England and America as free or placed in a new intermediate category. Again, Tocqueville portrays Amerindian society as free and egalitarian but inclusion of Indian tribes in the typology with advanced societies would be problematic.

Figure 1 is classificatory, not explanatory. By dichotomizing freedom-tyranny we can represent the causes of freedom and tyranny as indicated in Figure 2. Figure 3 links this theoretical structure to Tocqueville's typology of society. In Figure 3, arrow 1 identifies movement that Tocqueville thinks is inevitable (the democratic revolution), arrow 3 a movement he feared as all too likely. On the other hand, the blocked arrows ($\rightarrow$|) identify movements Tocqueville largely ruled out (arrow 2) or viewed as difficult (arrow 4). A society loses freedom (arrow 3) simply by failing to energetically protect it (1969: 504), which is precisely what happened in France (1955). *Recollections* and the sequel (1968b: 29-172) to *The Old Regime* describe France's continuing and unsuccessful attempts to regain it. Once freedom is lost, egoism, centralized administration, and force make its recapture difficult. In the modern world to these obstacles must be added those threats to freedom present even in free democracy: individualism, materialism, the affinity between equality and centralization, the preference for equality over freedom, and the tyranny of the majority. The line separating freedom and tyranny is differentially permeable; movement down is easier than movement up.

Treated separately, Parts A and B of Figure 2 might appear to represent configurations that invariably perpetuate themselves. Though Tocqueville feels that tyranny is a tunnel that once entered is difficult to exit, such is not the case. Law, order, rights, and aristocratic and municipal freedoms grew with the development of feudal society which, originating in conquest, was initially based on force. *The Old Regime* describes France's movement from freedom to tyranny (Figure 1); the

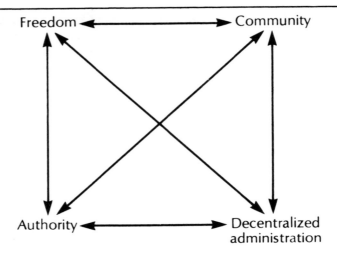

A. Freedom

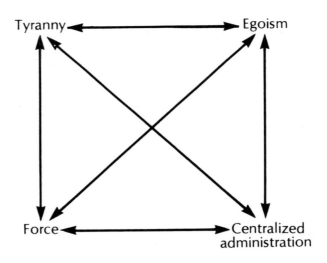

B. Tyranny

Figure 2   Tocqueville's Theory of Freedom

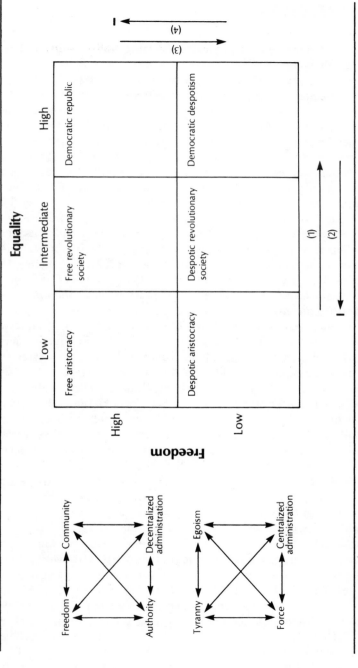

Figure 3   Tocqueville's Typology of Society and Theoretical Structure

61

underlying purpose of Tocqueville's writing was to help the French increase their freedom.

Though they are Tocqueville's two primordial variables, neither freedom nor equality is simply an independent or dependent variable. In that his is a theory of freedom, this is Tocqueville's main dependent variable; nonetheless, in relation to other key variables freedom is an independent variable (1955: xiii-xiv, 81). Freedom is reciprocally causally related to Tocqueville's other major causal variables (Figure 2).

Inequality-equality of conditions occupies a central place in Tocqueville's thinking. *The Old Regime* provides a detailed, historically specific account of the transition from inequality to equality. *Democracy* (1969: 9-12) offers a general account of this same transition and the factors promoting the development of equality. Beyond that, it details equality's effects. Although it appeared without subtitle, in a letter to Mill shortly before its publication, Tocqueville (1862, 2: 57; Schleifer, 1980: 34, 301) identified the title to Volume 2 of *Democracy* as *L'Influence de l'égalité sur les idées et les sentiments des hommes (The influence of equality on the ideas and sentiments of mankind)*. Altogether, Tocqueville is the preeminent sociologist of equality. Even so, Tocqueville's primary concern is freedom. Much of his interest in equality derives from its relationship to freedom. Tocqueville sees the obstacles to despotism posed by inequality and diversity in contrast to the affinity between equality and tyranny. However, although specific values of any one of Tocqueville's other major variables are linked causally to specific values of the others (Figure 2), each displays a full range of variation regardless of the level of equality (Figure 3). Nonetheless, equality remains fundamental. The level of equality constitutes the decisive variable aspect of the context for the other variables in Tocqueville's theory. Abstracted from this context it is possible to assert the relationships in Figure 2; but once these variables are applied empirically to and interpreted in terms of historically given societies, equality affects the variables themselves and their mutual relations.

Nowhere is this more evident than in the case of freedom. Its very meaning or, more exactly, how much of the society is free varies depending on the type of society. Free aristocratic societies possess an oligarchic and feudal freedom (1968b: 45-46; 1955: 17; 1968b: 45-46, 80; 1862, 1: 405), which was "often opposed to the freedom of individuals" (1969: 312). As in France's old regime, this freedom is an intermittent one that, limited to the higher classes and linked to immunity and privilege, "never went so far as to ensure even the most natural and essential rights to all alike" (1955: 119). The power of the aristocracy enables it to perpetuate its freedom and local control. The arbitrariness of the lords' treatment of those subject to their jurisdiction is constrained by morality, tradition, law, and community. Towns are largely self-governing. Secondary institutions balance the power of the government and provide protection from it. Such societies are freer than despotic aristocratic societies, where morality, custom, law, and community do not restrain the arbitrary treatment of inferiors by superiors; where towns and intermediate institutions, having lost their independence and power, are controlled by the central government; and where in rural areas centralized administration replaces the aristocracy as the governing authority. There is greater freedom in a free than in a despotic aristocratic society, even though by the standards of modern liberal society that freedom is unevenly spread and only a minority—particularly the king, the aristocracy, judges, the clergy, and the townspeople—are free. In contrast, freedom in modern democratic society exists to the extent that everyone (prisoners excepted) is free.

Other variables are also affected by the level of equality. In free aristocratic society authority is traditional, and subordination is the price the peasantry pays for protection and community. In free democratic society authority is based on the sovereignty of the people; classes are not hierarchically structured; and interclass community is based not on inequality, deference, and privilege but rather on the voluntary interaction and cooperation among individuals who, though differentially located in the social order, are free to move down or up in it. In tyrannical aristocratic society administrative techniques have yet to be perfected so that governmental tyranny is less pervasive than in democratic society. Lack of community appears as group individualism or egoism. In democratic despotism the perfection of administrative techniques permits the government to apply great force everywhere, even to the degree of penetrating individuals and controlling their wills. Lack of community appears not only as egoism but also as individualism and materialism.

Causal Relations

Tocqueville assumes people's willingness to coerce each other. Their virtue does not grow proportionately with their power; to the contrary, significant concentrations of unbalanced power destroy freedom because in such cases their power surpasses their wisdom and their justice (1969: 252). The only way to check power and, in the case of government, to prevent its inevitable attempts to monopolize power (1955: 58), is with another power. Accordingly, Tocqueville seeks to specify the conditions under which the central government's power is balanced and checked.

Decentralization, Community, and Freedom.[6] "Men's affections are drawn only in directions where power exists" (1969: 68). People give their resources and commitments to and identify with structures to the extent that doing so meets their needs and promotes their interests. Again, they participate in institutions to the extent that the institutions are functional for them (1969: 68-70; 1955: 45). Decentralized administration means that if individuals are to promote their interests and get things done—build and operate a school, church, or hospital, establish zoning laws, disseminate cherished values and beliefs, maintain law and order, promote local prosperity, protect local freedom—they have to act on their own initiative. Individuals seek each other out to accomplish collectively what would be impossible individually. Self-interest induces people to offer help to receive it in turn when they need it. They establish relationships and structures furthering their interests. Their interaction creates bonds linking them and creates a sense of mutual concern. In regular contact with one another, aware of each other's needs, mutually concerned, in the habit of working cooperatively, and having developed associational skills, people cooperate and maintain groups and structures to promote individual and collective interests. Decentralization leads to community, and community means that people are locally organized and active on behalf of their interests.

Decentralization and community mean that people are used to doing things for themselves and to acting cooperatively on their own behalf. Preferring to maintain their local self-determination, they use their skills and other resources to perpetuate the structures promoting their interests, including that in local autonomy. These structures provide the basis for resisting government attempts to dominate them. Decentralization and community, and the doctrine of the sovereignty of the people and the modern, democratic conception of liberty, mutually reinforce each other. Both structurally and ideologically decentralization and community promote effective resistance to outside control and perpetuate the bases of freedom.

Freedom encourages community and decentralization. Free from outside control people must do things for themselves if they are to be done. They seek each other out and work together cooperatively to promote their interests. Freedom not only *permits* but also *necessitates* the contact, locally organized activities, and controlled structures that mark decentralization and community.

Centralization, Egoism, and Tyranny. Centralization of administration discourages, as futile and irrational, participation in the many

---

6. To facilitate discussion of Tocqueville's theory we consider the links (Figure 2) among three variables before introducing the fourth (authority-force).

institutions controlled by it, including local government itself. Less attuned to local contingencies, centrally directed institutions are less responsive to local interests and needs. Consequently, people see less reason to become involved in them. Rather than participating actively in, controlling, making it responsive to their wishes, and identifying with local (and, ultimately, national) government as their own work, people are estranged from it and view it as an outsider. Nor do they attempt to create local institutions free from government control. Given government structures ostensibly designed to meet their needs, people see less reason to establish a parallel set of new structures. Rather than making the considerable effort necessary to do so, they take the easier path of working through existing institutions showing the subservience intended to induce a favorable government response to their egoistically motivated requests. For its part the government encourages this response by discouraging or prohibiting the exercise of power by institutions it does not control. Under these conditions people do not seek each other out and cooperatively maintain locally controlled institutions. Less in contact with one another, they are not mutually linked, and they lack mutual concern. Their egoism and lack of organization leave them divided, weak, and unable to effectively oppose the tyrannical power of a centralized administration.

Authority-Force and Freedom. Authority is a requisite both for orderly social life itself and for freedom (1969: 72; 238). Tocqueville (1969: 46) endorses Puritan leader John Winthrop's definition that distinguishes two types of liberty. The first, rejecting all authority, leads to license and disorder; in contrast, the second embraces legitimate authority as a sine qua non of liberty. Tocqueville (1862, 2: 39-40) evaluates governments in terms of their ability to promote liberty and human dignity. In analyzing the relationship between government and liberty he thinks of freedom less as freedom from external control and more as entailing both subjection to necessary authority and freedom from arbitrary and tyrannical control, that is, freedom from force.

The relationship between a government and its people can be thought of as an exchange (1955: 30; 1968b: 73). A government's power, privileged position, and inevitable extractions (for example, taxes) are earned to the degree that what it gets from the people is commensurate with the protection and other services it provides to meet their needs. By perpetuating what is perceived as a reasonable exchange the government generates authority. That authority is undermined when it fails to meet the people's needs or demands too much in return for services rendered or otherwise fails to meet the terms of reasonable exchange. The more a government's authority proves insufficient to permit it to do as it chooses, the more it will want to use force.

The decentralization-community-freedom configuration reduces the central government's power and thereby protects individuals from its encroachments on their freedom. This configuration also encourages the government to forgo the use of force as counterproductive, both because it is ineffective and because it undermines the government's authority and therefore its power. In forgoing the use of force and in relying on, protecting, and perhaps enhancing its authority, the government perpetuates that authority and the people's freedom.

Without a centralized administration government largely lacks the means of applying force. Community means multiple organized groups and secondary institutions diffused throughout the society that balance the administration's power and oppose its use of force. Community also means that, committed to the public good, people take an interest in public affairs, watch the government, support it where it promotes community interests, and oppose it where it encroaches on those interests or exceeds its authority. Freedom means an independent judiciary and free public opinion. The judiciary endorses the government's use of legitimate power, thereby adding the weight of the judicial system and law to the government's authority. Where the government employs force or otherwise exceeds its authority, the courts, by declaring laws or acts illegal, undermine that authority. Free public opinion and its associated institutions—such as a free press—generate a sustained flow of information. Subjecting the government to the glare of publicity, they bring it to the bar of public opinion. They inform the government when it fails to meet the people's needs or otherwise risks losing their allegiance. This flow of information helps the government increase its responsiveness and effectiveness and, consequently its authority. The press also mobilizes support for legitimate government action, pressures the government to meet the people's needs, and mobilizes opposition to its use of force (Figure 4, Part A).

Centralized administration gives the government the means of applying force. The major limitation on its power is the efficiency and responsiveness of its administrative apparatus. The lack of community means that it does not face organized centers of opposition. Even as the government becomes increasingly powerful through practice and improvements in administrative techniques, the people become increasingly accustomed to being dominated. Subjected to the government's power and the increasing disparity between its power and their will and ability to resist effectively, the people are easier to conquer as they become ever more egoistic, divided, and weak.

The government subjects everyone to the same laws, rules, and administrative procedures. Uniformly applied, these are not tailored to local and individual differences. Without a free press, free public opinion, and

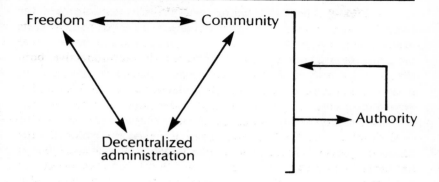

A. Freedom and authority

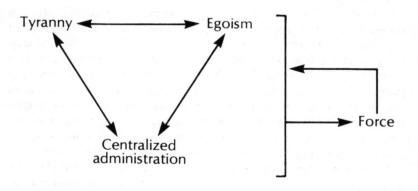

B. Tyranny and force

Figure 4 Freedom and Authority-Force

the free flow of information, the government's understanding of the opinions and interests of the governed is reduced. It relies increasingly on its own official mechanisms to keep informed, mechanisms that produce distorted, inadequate information about the people's sentiments and interests. The government seeks to promote prosperity and otherwise help its people. However, even its well-intentioned policies typically fail to accord with the people's sentiments or to meet their needs. Removed from the glare of free public opinion and the control of publicity, the government often acts in secrecy. Its failure to stay close to the governed and attuned to their needs undermines its success in meeting their needs, which in turn undermines its authority. Instead, it is viewed increasingly as a remote, oppressive stranger.

Controlled by the government, a subservient judiciary endorses its acts, declaring the arbitrary and illegal legal. At the extreme, legal scholars appear "to prove that violence is lawful . . . that the defeated have been guilty," and "that Terror is Law, that Tyranny equals Order, that Servitude means Progress" (1968b: 151, 155). Free of judicial control, the government's use of power surpasses traditional and legal limits, which further undermines its authority. Altogether the government increasingly monopolizes power, frees itself from external control, exceeds and undermines its authority, destroys community, relies on appeals to the egoism of a weak, subjugated, atomized populace and, where that fails, on force (Figure 4, Part B).

Though Tocqueville typically employs a society as his unit of analysis, we may also apply his theory to the local community in feudal or free aristocratic society. In terms of his basic theoretical structure (Figure 2), these communities represent a mixed theoretical configuration (1968b: 45). Instead of the decentralized administration found at the national level, local government is dominated by an aristocrat who exercises his power in a somewhat arbitrary and tyrannical fashion. Peasants and their lords interact. Peasants provide personal household and other services for lords. Their governing functions bring lords into sometimes cooperative contact with the peasantry. Lords supervise the peasantry both to ensure that peasants provide them with traditional goods and services and because their power depends on the prosperity of the local community. The lord has some concern for the welfare of all those who, as members of the community, are subject to his jurisdiction. In return for their service and subservience peasants receive protection and some aid during times of scarcity. Governed by tradition, this unequal exchange legitimates the lord's power.

This combination of concentrated power, traditional authority, and interclass community produces both freedom and tyranny. Lords are free but this freedom results from the decentralized national administration coupled with the lord's dominance at the local level. The very localness of government increases its knowledge of and ability to be responsive to local conditions. Lord-peasant interaction creates community, but their mutual empathy is undermined by the inequality that separates them. The presence of traditional authority and the community of unequals provides peasants with little freedom but nonetheless more freedom than they experience when authority is replaced by force and community by egoism.

   A Core. Two causal chains lie at the core of Tocqueville's theory (Figure 5). People interact to the degree that doing so meets their interests (Figure 5, Part A). Interaction creates community; it generates mutual concern and through it people maintain the institutions in which they participate, that they control, that meet their interests, and that give them the will and the resources necessary to resist administrative centralization and unwelcome government interference in their lives. Free, they prefer to remain so. Their freedom creates the necessity to interact in order to maintain those structures that further their interests. On the other hand, where a despotic government dominates local institutions, people lack the interests motivating interaction (Figure 5, Part B). There is no community, either structurally or social psychologically, and egoism prevails. People lack both that mutual concern that becomes concern for the public interest and the organizational resources necessary to oppose administrative centralization and its tyrannical control of their lives. Indeed, with government the only active agency capable of helping them meet many of their interests, people seek its help, not to promote the common interests of the larger community but for their egoistically defined self-interest. Their requests for help are accompanied by the obsequiousness intended to induce a favorable governmental response. The government uses its centralized administration to keep the people divided, weak, egoistic, and devoid of the organizational resources or even the will to actively oppose its imposition of tyranny. Together, these conditions enable a powerful government to pursue successfully a divide-and-conquer strategy.

Additional Variables

   Energy-Activity and Prosperity. Tocqueville's explanation of a people's energy-activity level overlaps with his theory of freedom. The greater the administrative centralization and the more the central government intervenes in and controls their lives, the less reason people see to act on their own behalf, the less opportunity they have to do so, and the less likely their efforts are to produce satisfactory results. Less used to providing for themselves, people are more used to waiting for government intervention and help. Conversely, the greater the decentralization and the less the government does, the more people do for themselves, both individually and cooperatively. The character traits,

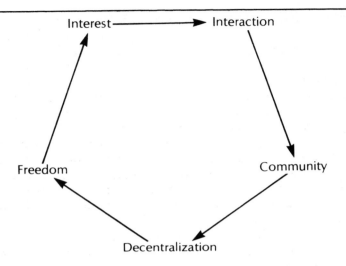

A. Freedom

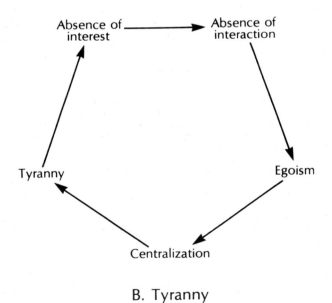

B. Tyranny

Figure 5   Tocqueville's Theory: A Core

habits, and mores that permit despotism and that it promotes undermine energy-activity; on the other hand, those that engender freedom
and that freedom engenders also promote energy-activity.[7]

Tocqueville's explanation turns on the inverse relationship between
the extent of governmental and individual action. The number of people
outside government and the sum of their activity far exceed the number
in the government and the sum of its activity. Consequently, the people's
energy-activity level is decisive (1969: 88, 92-93, 97, 223-224; 1955: 42,
123; 1968b: 167). In some societies the centralization is as omnipresent
as the lethargy it produces; in others, for example, America, the agency
directing social life is as invisible as the constant activity is apparent
(1969: 72). The contrast between free and despotic countries is striking:
"there, all is activity and bustle; here all seems calm and immobile"
(1969: 242; see also 1836: 90).[8]

In addition to influencing a nation's greatness, energetic activity is the
basic source of a people's social and economic prosperity. Tocqueville
repeatedly cites comparisons showing that despotism reduces and freedom promotes energy and prosperity (1969: 209). England and America
surpass France in freedom and prosperity. French Canada's centralization, itself an extension of French institutions, and lack of prosperity
contrasts with the freedom and prosperity of America as an inheritance
of her English heritage (1955: 253-254). Similarly, *The Old Regime's*
appendix (1955: 212-221) contrasts Languedoc's greater freedom and
prosperity with that found in the rest of France.

---

7. *Journeys to England and Ireland* (1968a: 105-106; see also 1969: 402-404) uses these perspectives
to explain the more specific relationship between freedom and commerce, particularly manufacturing
and trade. Agreeing with Montesquieu that "the spirit of trade naturally gives men the spirit of liberty,"
Tocqueville feels there is an even stronger influence in the opposite direction. Though some free peoples
have been neither manufacturers nor traders, he cites Phoenicians, medieval Italians, and others in
support of his observation that he knows of no example of a trading people who have not been free.
Freedom requires general alertness, planning and perseverance in executing difficult tasks, independence, and tolerance of agitation, change, and danger. All the things—the spirit, character traits,
habits, and mores—that engender freedom "are equally needed for success in commerce."

8. Tocqueville (1862, 1: 346) also observes that liberty promotes the very materialism that can
undermine both liberty and one of its chief sources, religion. Especially in modern times, if liberty is to
perpetuate itself it needs the support not only of religion, morality, and community, but also the
support engendered by widespread recognition of its links to prosperity.

Tocqueville's application of these perspectives to America—"time and prosperity have there
deprived the religious element of three fourths of its original power"—may be compared to John
Wesley as quoted by Weber (1958b: 175):

Wherever riches have increased, the essence of religion has decreased in the same proportion.
Therefore I do not see how it is possbile . . . for any revival of true religion to continue long. For
religion must necessarily produce both industry and frugality, and these cannot but produce
riches. But as riches increase, so will pride, anger, and love of the world in all its branches.

Wesley's proposed solution was to "*exhort all Christians to gain all they can, and to save all they can.*"

Tocqueville acknowledges that despotism and prosperity may coexist (1955: xiv, 168; 1968b: 167; 1969: 240) and that despotism may in the short-run be a better guarantee of prosperity than freedom (1955: 168); however, in the long-run freedom increases the energy and prosperity that despotism reduces.[9]

Equality also affects energy and prosperity. In ascriptive aristocratic society mobility is restricted. Locked into traditional stations and lifestyles and, governed by tradition, people are not concerned to move up in order to enjoy that which custom and society deny them. Aristocrats are generally wealthy; but even though they are concerned with money and economic prosperity, their codes of honor encourage them to subordinate this concern to such aristocratic values as courage, loyalty, and military valor (1969: 617-619). In contrast, the materialism of democratic society induces restless, energetic pursuit of the prosperity that is potentially available to all that permits people to gratify their materialistic desires. In sum, despotic aristocracy is the least energetic and prosperous type of society, a free democracy the most prosperous. As mixed types, free aristocracy and despotic democracy fall between these extremes.

Religion and Morality. Tocqueville asserts an intimate link among religion, morality, and freedom. Liberty presupposes morality and morality religion (1969: 17, 47, 294). Human greatness is maximized when liberty animates and religion restrains behavior (1862, 2: 230).

Religion is a source of worldview and morality (1968b: 304). Tocqueville evaluated religions in terms of the degree to which they taught the values to which he himself subscribed. Born and raised a Catholic, he espoused the basic moral truths of Christianity and often equated it with civilization and its progress generally. However, if most religions are beneficial, there are exceptions: the source of "morbid consequences," Mohammedanism has had an immense, generally pernicious influence on the human race (1968b: 212; 1862, 1: 325-326).

Historically, Christianity is responsible for three major changes in morality (1968b: 190-194). Tocqueville (1862, 2: 328) distinguishes two types of morality, private and public. In terms of this division between the milder, Christian, or private virtues such as neighborly love, forgivingness, justice, and temperance (1862, 2: 317) and public virtues, the morality of the classic societies and Christian morality are mirror images of each other. The only weakness of Christianity was its neglect

---

9. Tocqueville (1969: 94) disagrees with one of his great mentors— "I pass a short portion of every day with three men, Pascal, Montesquieu, and Rousseau" (1862, 1: 312-313)—on the effects of despotism: "Montesquieu, in attributing a peculiar force to despotism, did it an honor which, I think, it did not deserve. Despotism by itself can maintain nothing durable. When one looks close, one sees that what made absolute governments long prosperous was religion, not fear."

of public virtue just as classic morality's emphasis on such virtue was its only strength. If this first change in morality—greater emphasis on private and less emphasis on public virtues—wrought by Christianity represented its only significant backward step, the other two changes were unmixed advances. By putting moral sanction and the ultimate aim of life in the afterlife instead of in this world, Christianity gave morality a more spiritual, altruistic, higher character. Finally, whereas the older moral systems were limited to specific groups and in endorsing even extreme inequality legitimated such evils as slavery, Christianity asserted the equality, unity, and community of all men. Although each of these three doctrines existed prior to it, Christianity integrated them into a religious morality that captivated the human mind. Christianity's "grand achievement" as a moral system "is to have formed a human community beyond national societies" (1968b: 192).

Having identified the two decisive innovations in contemporary morality, Tocqueville (1968b: 193-194) interprets them as basic Christian principles in modern dress. First, Christianity asserted the equality of all men in the spiritual realm; modern morality gives them equal rights in the material realm. Together with extensions of wealth, education, and the other developments in the democratic revolution that have increased equality, Christianity has established the principle that everyone is entitled to certain basic goods and pleasures, and that everyone is morally obligated to see that no one lacks life's necessities. Second, Christianity's definition of charity as a personal virtue—those with more are morally obligated to help those who have less—has become defined as a social and political duty, as a public virtue. In the modern world more and more people turn to the government to meet an increasing number of their needs, even as it assumes responsibility for redressing unacceptable inequalities and assisting the unfortunate (1968b: 193). A century and a half after Tocqueville we recognize this modern morality as the morality of the welfare state.

Religious beliefs are influenced by the social structure and the place of the church (or churches) in that structure. Kings and priests have used religion as a weapon to promote their own interests (1968b: 205). Through all the worldly vicissitudes to which it has been subjected, Christianity has shown its ability to endure inequality and equality, peace and war, prosperity and depression, empire and political fragmentation, political and religious revolution, and the transition to the modern world. If temporarily subverted from time to time, Christianity and its moral truths are an enduring influence that constitute the foundation of contemporary morality (1968b: 208).

Christianity leads people from materialism to spiritual values and concerns. It teaches them to think not only of this-worldly rewards but also of the sanctions in the next, and that worldly injustice will be rectified in the afterlife. By instructing them about their duties to one another it reduces their egoism. If its assertion of the equality of all people has given impetus to the democratic revolution, Christianity combats democracy's congenital vices: materialism and individualism.

Religions remain truer to their religious mission when they are able to perpetuate separation between church and state and avoid political entanglements and authority. Ardently desiring religious renewal in France, Tocqueville (1862, 2: 170-171) felt that direct government action designed to bring this about would be counterproductive. Rather, religious rebirth would occur only to the extent that their individual experiences made people feel the need for it. An understanding of the conditions and consequences of faith encouraged people to promote religion. Tocqueville repeatedly noted that, possessed with this understanding, the Americans supported it for pragmatic reasons. In France first the upper class, then the middle, and finally even those sections of the lower class with material possessions came to support religion for its pragmatic value as a protection against revolution (1968b: 154; 1955: 154). However, the moralist's, writer's, philosopher's, historian's, or politician's ability to bring about the religious rebirth of a nation was circumscribed. To have maximum effect, to be practically prescriptive as opposed to simply being descriptive and analytic, Tocqueville had to identify alternative sources of the morality that would promote his cherished values.

Patriotism and religion are the only sources of the "free concurrence" of wills that generate that exceptional power among people, which is capable of making everyone ardently pursue the same goal (1969: 94). Along with freedom and religion, patriotism, itself "a sort of religion" (1969: 235), is a great mover of people. Basic to patriotism (1969: 235-237; 1968b: 34) are the mores that explain its power. The greatest malady menacing Tocqueville's France was the degradation of spirit, the mediocrity of tastes, and the degeneration of mores (1954: 335). Especially under these conditions a nation must cultivate the feelings that inspire great actions. "The most elevated feeling now left to us is national pride" (1862, 2: 69). Patriotism and nationalism can supplant the lethargy, individualism, and materialism that Tocqueville so detested in the public spirit. However, patriotism is potentially dangerous. Foreign threats or the prospect of military victory may arouse it, but when international conflict escalated beyond diplomatic confrontation to war the cost in death and destruction was high. As a source of militarization patriotism also promotes the centralization and despotism from which France already suffered.

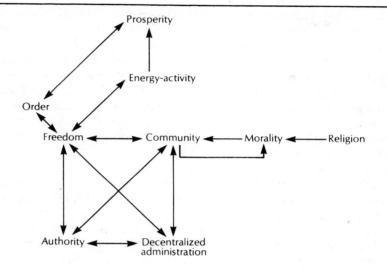

A. Freedom and its correlates

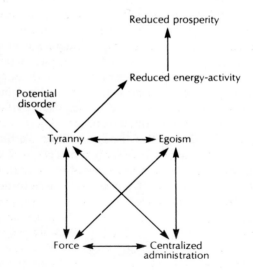

B. Tyranny and its correlates

Figure 6   Tocqueville's Theory: Additional Variables and Causal Relationships

Religious renewal was beyond legislative enactment, and the effects of intense patriotism were mixed. Even while seeking to understand each, Tocqueville had reason to identify other means of promoting his values. Interaction generates the mutual concern that Tocqueville valued in itself. However, it was not enough that people possess private virtue and be "good fathers, honest merchants, exemplary landowners, and good Christians" (1955: xiv). They must also be concerned with the local and the national welfare. Tocqueville's wish to encourage people to promote public virtue (community) and freedom underlies his theorizing.

Order-Disorder. If freedom presupposes order, freedom is itself a source of order. Recognizing that disorder impedes their pursuits, people, especially a free, energetic, prosperous people whose multiple activities presuppose order, demand it of the government.

The order of tyrannical society differs from that of free society. In a free society people control the institutions in which they participate, identify with them as their own work, and submit to authority as a necessity. They resist disorder as a threat to the institutions to which they are committed.

Lacking adequate authority, tyrannical governments use force. People submit to the government's greater force less because they feel it has a right to issue binding directives than because they fear reprisals, and for this and other reasons find it more convenient to submit than to resist. The failure of institutions to meet their needs undermines commitment to them. Because the government demands more than it returns and fails to promote their interests, and because people prefer freedom to tyranny, there is latent opposition to the government. Liberty presupposes and promotes order; even when successfully imposing surface order, tyranny simultaneously creates potential disorder.

Figure 6 includes the additional variables discussed above. Tocqueville also addresses many other variables. The strength of Tocqueville's theory lies not only in the core on which I have focused but also in its inclusiveness and potential for development, a potential that has yet to be fully realized.

3

Comparison with Marx and Durkheim

Theories exist in a world of mutual supplementation but also of competition and reciprocal critique. Having stated Tocqueville's theory, I now propose to compare him to other preeminent social theorists. Consideration of one consensus theorist, Durkheim, and one conflict theorist, Marx, will allow us to consider important differences between these two traditions. Recognizing that comparison with either Marx or Weber could be equally instructive, I have selected Marx, because his sharper divergence from Tocqueville highlights important aspects of the latter's theoretical contribution.

MARX

Economic Structure of Society

In 1859 Marx (1972: 4-5) formulated some general conclusions that guided his studies. Relations of production or the economic structure of society constitutes "the real foundation, on which rises a legal and political superstructure and to which correspond definite forms of social consciousness. The mode of production of material life conditions the social, political and intellectual life process in general." Furthermore, major social transformations occur as a result of development of society's productive forces, which brings about new relations of production and eventually leads to a transformation of the superstructure.

In contrast to Marx's emphasis on society's economic structure a recurring criticism of Tocqueville is that he neglected economic factors. Richter (1967: 118) asserts that Tocqueville failed "to concern himself systematically with economic phenomena." Second on Pierson's (1938: 764) list of *Democracy's* "serious blunders" is Tocqueville's "neglect of American material development. Some critics would call this Tocqueville's greatest blind spot." Herr (1962: 120-121) lists errors in *The Old Regime* related to Tocqueville's "lack of interest in economic questions." Both *Democracy* and *The Old Regime* paid inadequate attention to economic factors, according to Goldstein (1975: 123).

Notwithstanding the chorus of criticism, the economic dimension is integral to Tocqueville's definition of his problem. His concern for morality directs his attention to whatever threatens it. Although he recognizes that, like other interests, the pursuit of economic interests could lead to contact and community, analytically he links the economic sphere to egoism. Given his desire to promote community, public virtue, justice, and freedom, Tocqueville is concerned by the threat posed to all of these by economic interests, values, and institutions.

Two letters state an analytical starting point in the development of Tocqueville's explanation of freedom in America. Containing impressions formed within a month of his arrival, these letters reflect his thinking long before *Democracy* appeared. In democratic society, aristocratic society's political, social, economic, and ideological ties of domination and community were broken, leaving individuals isolated and equal. Whereas in democratic France "the government concerns itself with everything," in America "there is, or appears to be, no government" (Tocqueville, letter to his father, quoted in Pierson, 1938: 114-115). What, then, rules society and integrates the diverse elements constituting America? What makes them a people? "Interest? There lies the secret. Private interest crops up at every moment, and indeed it vaunts itself openly, proclaiming itself as a social theory" (1966: 731). The materialism of democratic society reinforces economic interests. Given his analytic image of democratic society as an individualistic, materialistic collection of equal, atomized individuals, Tocqueville seeks the factors which, preventing Americans from falling into disorder and losing their freedom, instead made them a free, prosperous, integrated people. *Democracy* details his answer. It considers the causes and impact of economic cycles in democratic society; "why Americans consider all honest callings honorable" (1969: 550-551); "what gives almost all Americans a preference for industrial callings" (551-554);

"how democratic institutions and mores tend to raise rent and shorten the terms of leases" (580-582); and the "influence of democracy on wages" (582-584). He shows: "how the Americans combat the effects of individualism by free institutions" (509-513) "how the Americans combat individualism by the doctrine of self-interest properly understood" (525-528); "how in America the taste for physical pleasures is combined with love of freedom and attention to public affairs" (539-541); "how religious beliefs at times turn the thoughts of Americans toward spiritual things" (542-546); and "equality naturally gives men the taste for free institutions" (667-668). Tocqueville identifies the pluralistic distribution of economic power as an important source of American freedom. He shows how political, economic, and social associations mutually strengthen one another and how the ideas, habits, tastes, desires, interests and values of economic life are reciprocally causally related to those in noneconomic life.

A recurring motif in *The Old Regime* is the government's demand for ever more money and its resulting tax and other fiscal policies, which had a devastating impact on community. Tocqueville (1955: 173-174) argues that the two decades of prosperity preceding it helped bring about the French Revolution. The reassertion of the nobility's long-lapsed feudal economic privileges infuriated the peasants. By simultaneously encouraging and thwarting the people's materialistic desires the government helped seal its own doom (1955: 179). The increasing French propensity to treat each other in terms of individual economic benefit and evade political and other obligations destroyed community. All this contrasts with conditions in England where an economically, socially, and politically dominant aristocracy perpetuated community.

Tocqueville was ever concerned with political economy. *Democracy* treats free versus slave labor as the decisive difference between the North and South. Political economy is equally central to the contrast between aristocratic and democratic society. The former is a largely agrarian society in which the aristocracy's local dominance is at once political, economic, and social. In democratic society these dimensions become more empirically differentiated. In free aristocratic society the aristocracy's political and economic stake in the local community, leadership of that community, and concern for those they dominated are all intertwined. In free democratic societies community is perpetuated by the need to cooperate with others economically and otherwise to achieve collectively what is impossible individually.

Tocqueville observed that he lived in an age of transition in which the aristocratic values of power, glory, the grand, the heroic, and the morally uplifting were being replaced by a democratic, bourgeoisie mentality and values. Ruled by unenlightened self-interest and consumed by their preoccupation with money, comfort, and prosperity, people led petty, circumscribed lives. Industrialization and the rise of the middle class meant the rule of democratic economic values that debased people by subverting community, public virtue, and freedom (see also Boesche, 1981).

Causal Importance of Economic Factors. Although he assesses their importance, traces their effects, and analyzes their interaction with noneconomic factors, Tocqueville does not attribute causal primacy to economic factors in history and society. Other analysts do, of course, attribute varying amounts of causal primacy to economic and other material factors. Lenski and Lenski (1978) demonstrate the importance of technology as a determinant of sociocultural evolution. Using mode of subsistence to define four basic types of society—hunting and gathering, horticultural, agrarian, and industrial—they show how development from one type to another is determined by a society's ability to mobilize coded information, especially in the form of technology (Lenski and Lenski, 1978: 67, 89). Marx, opposing his materialism to idealism and beginning with the hypothesis of the importance of the material mode of production, seeks to show how changes in the means of production led, in Western European history, from primitive communism to ancient to feudal to capitalist society. He also seeks to show how a complex mix of developments in the economic structure of capitalist society will lead to future communism. Among these changes were a falling rate of profit and a cycle of increasingly severe boom and bust. Other changes also reflected the dialectical, irrational nature of capitalist society: class (including ideological) conflict, polarization, the ability to produce versus the ability to consume, rising productivity versus the impoverishment of the proletariat, those (the proletariat) who produce value get few social rewards while those (capitalists) who produce no value get the lion's share, the social character of production versus the private appropriation of profit, machines ostensibly designed to benefit people instead enslave them, and labor exists for production instead of the reverse.

Though they emphasize the importance of technology, in specifying its causal limits Lenski and Lenski state a position consistent with Tocqueville.[1] Technology is exceedingly important. "First, it determines

---

1. Lenski and Lenski's (1978: 419-422) assessment of levels of different kinds of freedom for elites and nonelites is similar to Tocqueville's. They feel that for the average members of society the level of freedom declines from hunting and gathering to horticultural to agrarian society after which it increases substantially in industrial societies to a level surpassing that in hunting and gathering society. Tocqueville (1969: 28-29) views the American Indians as free, sees greatly reduced freedom for feudal serfs, somewhat greater freedom for peasants in aristocratic society, and still greater freedom for citizens in free democratic society.

the *range of what is possible*" for a society (preindustrial societies don't launch earth satellites). Second, "technology determines *the relative costs* of" options, "that is, the relative costs of the things within [a society's] 'range of the possible'" (1978: 69). But Lenski and Lenski are equally careful to note that, of course, "technology does not determine all a society's characteristics." Technologically similar societies vary greatly. Such economic (material) factors as mode of production and technology do not answer Tocqueville's question because they do not explain variation in freedom in societies that are economically similar.

Tocqueville's comparisons sustained his assessment of the importance of economic phenomena. England and France in the centuries immediately preceding the industrial revolution demonstrated that aristocratic societies employing the same technology may differ in freedom. England was freer than France, not because of differences in the way the two countries materially produced, but because of different political and social structures. With a powerful aristocracy, decentralized administration, community, and authority, England was free. Characterized by centralized administration, egoism, force, and an aristocracy largely shorn of local political power, France was despotic. Nor in Tocqueville's day did industrialization explain differences in freedom. England was the most industrialized, and the United States the least; yet England and America were free but France was not. Not economic development but other aspects of the past as they influence the present (England versus France) and circumstances of birth (America) explained tyranny-freedom.

Twentieth-century comparisons further sustain Tocqueville's perspective on the importance of economic factors. Germany shows that an advanced industrialized state may be transformed from democracy to fascism and back to democracy and Japan provides another illustration of the change from fascism to democracy. Of course, war and its aftermath were instrumental in these transformations. Having been Foreign Minister of France for five months himself (June-October, 1849), Tocqueville recognized the importance of international relations and how one nation may affect the course of history in another. He noted how, through the power of ideology and military conquest, the French Revolution and its aftermath influenced individual European governments and societies and, indeed, the fate of Europe, generally. Again, in the contemporary world nations with advanced means of production vary greatly socially, politically, and culturally just as nations with relatively underdeveloped means of production display an equally wide range of noneconomic variation. Neither technology nor means of production determine relations of production, the superstructure, or level of freedom.

Economic variables occupy a place in Tocqueville's theory analogous to that of inequality-equality. Though generally not itself a decisive cause of freedom or tyranny, level of equality is a decisive aspect of the context in which tyranny and freedom exist, and extreme, permanent inequality engenders tyrannical treatment of inferiors by their superiors (Tocqueville, 1968b: 229). Similarly, for Tocqueville, Marx's forces of production do not determine the relations of production and societies with a similar economic structure may vary greatly socially, politically, and culturally. In short, base does not determine superstructure. Nonetheless, the economic structure of society is important not only in its own right but also as a factor that interacts with and affects the noneconomic factors in terms of which Tocqueville seeks to explain freedom. And like those in other spheres, unbalanced concentrations of economic power (for example, industrialists) are tyrannical.

Class, Class Hegemony, and Class Conflict

Ironically, Marx's (1972: 4-5) famous summary statement of historical materialism in the Preface to *A Contribution to the Critique of Political Economy* does not explicitly mention class and class conflict, which itself invites speculation on the reception that such a summary statement by anyone other than Marx would have received had it omitted these basic concepts. Marx supplemented his base-superstructure model of society with a class model (see, for example, Marx, 1972: 335-362, 436-525). One point of articulation between the two models is that Marx defines class in terms of relationship to the means of production. Treating society as a hierarchically structured system of power, both models seek to identify the bases of that power and the directions and consequences of its employment. The base-superstructure model asserts the primacy of the means of production. It directs attention to how they structure the relations of production, and how these two together as base influence the superstructure. Identifying control over the means of production as the basic source of social power, the class model of society asserts that the class with this control thereby becomes politically, socially, and culturally, including ideologically, dominant. Scarce and widely sought after, power is a zero-sum phenomenon the exercise of which produces opposition. The resulting class conflict is the driving force of social change and history.

From these perspectives we may derive two criticisms of Tocqueville. First, he fails to understand that control over the means of production confers power that is then translated into other forms of domination.

Second, he sometimes underestimates the importance of class and class conflict.

Rejecting the economic reductionism that asserts economic power to be the ultimate source of social power, Tocqueville distinguishes four types of power: social, economic, political, and ideological (control over ideas) or, more broadly, cultural. Each type must be analyzed not in terms of reducing any one to another but in terms of their relative importance, their mutual relations, the context established for each by all the others, and their changing relations in changing circumstances. Analyses incorporating this approach contain some of Tocqueville's greatest insights. The power of wealth is different in despotic (France) from that in free aristocracy (England) and different again in democracy (America). In France the former "ruling class," the aristocracy, was alienated from other classes as it retained privilege and status even while losing political power to the central administration. Prospering economically, the middle class was denied highest social status even though it dominated public administrative offices, and many in the middle class were wealthier than much of the aristocracy. This situation increased middle-class/nobility estrangement. Without political office, high social status, or wealth, public opinion leadership gave the French philosophers political power. *The Old Regime* is a classic demonstration of the gain achieved by refusing to reduce all forms of power to one type, economic or otherwise, and by analyzing the impact of changes in the distribution of different kinds of power and values as that affects internal group cohesion, relations between and among groups, and ultimately, the course of society and history.

The second criticism of Tocqueville is that he sometimes missed the importance of class and class conflict. The analysis in *The Old Regime* is consistent with Tocqueville's (1955: 122) assertion that to some may sound more Marxian than Tocquevillian: "I am dealing here with classes as a whole, to my mind the historian's proper study." However, Tocqueville defines class differently from Marx. Though relationship to means of production is a factor in class, and though individuals in the same class typically occupy the same relationship to the means of production, *The Old Regime* does not define class in these terms. Rather than use a criterion of class that assumes the primacy of one type of power, for example, economic power, *The Old Regime* treats classes as inclusive groups of people who see themselves and are seen by others as belonging together: for example, peasant, working class, middle class, and aristocracy. Though in comparing two people, one an aristocrat and the other middle class, there are instances in which they share a similar relationship to the means of production or in which the middle-class person is far wealthier, nonetheless aristocrats belong to the higher class.

If Tocqueville did not miss the importance of classes and class conflict in *The Old Regime,* he is held to have done so in *Democracy.* In explicit contrast to Tocqueville's portrayal of egalitarian America, Pessen (1978: 77-100) characterizes Jacksonian America as "the inegalitarian society." Pessen's treatment raises important issues. How can we decide whether a society is egalitarian? Tocqueville's concept of equality is inclusive. A society can be more egalitarian in some ways than in others. Is egalitarianism to be measured by the standard of perfect equality, in which case it will be easier to show inequality, or is it to be measured comparatively in terms of the contrast between aristocratic and democratic society or more and less egalitarian societies generally, in which case it will be easier to picture America as egalitarian? In studying America Tocqueville (1969: 19) sought more than America—he sought democracy itself. This makes it essential to distinguish between his empirical description of America and his analytic portrayal of egalitarian society. Finally, there is the hobgoblin of trends and hindsight. Did Tocqueville's analysis of aristocracy and democracy as polar opposites or his extrapolation of trends derived by contrasting aristocratic and democratic society color his empirical depiction of America? And, in turn, in assessing Tocqueville do we use trends or developments, less decisive or unambiguous then than now, to assess his portrayal?

Pessen (1978: 77-100; 1979) easily cites massive inequality in Jacksonian America. Great fortunes existed and the opulence of the rich rivaled that of their European counterparts (Pessen, 1978: 82). The urban working class led precarious lives burdened by low wages and the specter of unemployment (Pessen, 1978: 84). Agricultural laborers were paid still less than urban workers, and the life of even the moderately successful independent farmer was one of monotony, hard work, and generally poor quality (Pessen, 1978: 83). Instead of circulating rapidly, wealth remained concentrated in the same hands. Rates of social mobility were "dramatically slight" (Pessen, 1978: 90), making Tocqueville's belief in high rates of mobility "as false as . . . his belief in Jacksonian equality of condition" (Pessen, 1978: 86). More than 90% of the urban wealthy were descended from socially and economically elite families; only 2% were born poor (Pessen, 1978: 86). Defined by massive disparities in lifestyle, great social distance, exclusiveness, and strong barriers, clearly demarcated classes existed (Pessen, 1978: 92). Trends were the opposite of those postulated by Tocqueville, as wealth became progressively less evenly distributed from prerevolutionary to Jacksonian to mid-nineteenth-century America.

Though public officials had to compete for the common man's (white males') vote, nonetheless, the prosperous controlled offices at all levels of government and implemented party and government policies favoring the rich (Pessen, 1978: 97-99), and the wealthy dominated voluntary associations. Although working people sometimes organized to promote their interests, the ineffectiveness of these attempts simply demonstrated their powerlessness.

"All of the chief assumptions underlying the egalitarian thesis are undermined by" recent evidence (Pessen, 1978: 99). "Far from being an era of egalitarianism" Jacksonian America was "an age of inequality, whether in material condition, status, opportunity, or influence and power" (Pessen, 1978: 100). Indeed, "not equality but a general inequality of condition among the people was the 'central feature' of" that America (Pessen, 1978: 86). Though known as the "era of the common man" and the "age of egalitarianism" (Pessen, 1978: 77), "the *in*egalitarian society is becoming our new point of departure in our perception of antebellum America" (Pessen, 1979: 224). In sum, antebellum egalitarianism is a myth (Pessen, 1979; see also Pessen, 1982, and the literature cited therein).

To what extent does Pessen's portrayal necessitate modification of Tocqueville? The Frenchman (1969: 209) holds that any society can be divided into three classes: the rich, the moderately well-to-do, and the poor. Tocqueville also feels that America was egalitarian. What, then, is his view of classes in egalitarian society?

The concern with inequality produces endemic tension in a democratic society such as America. Anxious about their status and afraid of being leveled, people are concerned to distinguish themselves from and elevate themselves above their fellows (1969: 570). "There is no nobleman in Europe more exclusive in his pleasures or more jealous of the slightest advantages assured by a privileged position" than a wealthy American (1969: 179). People want others to be equal even as they want to elevate themselves above the crowd. Status anxiety and hatred of privilege and inequality increase even as privilege and inequality diminish (1969: 538, 672-673). Whereas in aristocratic society people are separated by visible, impenetrable barriers (Tocqueville, 1969: 605), in democratic society they are divided by weaker barriers that they strive to use to raise themselves above others but that they resent when others do the same to them.

Tocqueville does not deny American inequalities in class, status, political power, and education, or accompanying variation in ideas, tastes, habits, passions, interests, values, or lifestyles. Indeed, he contrasts classes in just such terms. However, he does assert that class differences and relations exist within an egalitarian framework. The vast majority work or are dependent on those who do, and all honest occupations are honorable. Moderate education is widespread; few people are either illiterate or highly educated. Mobility is extensive and wealth circulates rapidly. The rich, most of whom were once poor (1969: 532), fear becoming poor just as the poor aspire to wealth. If the rich are advantaged, nonetheless opportunity is widespread and the poor can, with luck and hard work, move up. Wealth and poverty constitute possibly temporary situations, not permanent inequality. Though the poor envy the rich and the rich prefer to associate with each other, egalitarian mores dictate that in public rich and poor treat each other not as inferior and superior, but as equals. The fluid class boundaries can, as when a poor person acquires wealth, be traversed. Class confers no hereditary or other special rights and privileges. Lower-class people do not expect to defer in opinion or otherwise to higher classes. Egalitarian values reign and inequalities inconsistent with them are subject to constant attack and erosion. All people are equal before the law and most men have acquired the right to vote and to compete for even the highest public offices. The people are sovereign and authority derives from the consent of the governed. Though the wealthy have the advantages and power of wealth, and however much they privately disdain the people, nonetheless they too share middle-class values and must bow before the tyranny of the majority. Notwithstanding its three classes and significant class differences, most Americans are of meager wealth and America is predominantly a middle-class society.

To the extent that his account is factually accurate—Pessen (1979: 224) stresses that only further research will permit a definitive account of antebellum America—Tocqueville's portrait must be revised. The circulation of wealth was restricted, not rapid. Most rich were not formerly poor. There was greater inheritance of social and economic position than Tocqueville asserted. The opportunity structure was more restricted and fewer Americans were able to take advantage of it and move up than Tocqueville thought. Many Americans were poor. Tocqueville overestimated the middle while underestimating the opulence of the rich and the extent of poverty. Government, powerful voluntary associations, and other power structures were dominated not by the common person but by the wealthy.

Clearly, then, America was less egalitarian than Tocqueville thought. Equally clearly, with the obvious exception of the South, Blacks, Indians, and, in a different way, women (1969: 590-594, 600-603), analyzed in terms of the aristocratic-democratic society comparison in many ways America was indeed egalitarian. All men were held to have been created free and equal and to be equal before God. Patterns of class deference were weak. There was no legal or other impenetrable barriers to upward or downward mobility. Those who prospered could often themselves gain partial and their children full acceptance in higher circles. Rather than being taught to accept their place in society, people were encouraged to aspire to the top. Americans believed that opportunity was widespread and in the possibility of upward mobility for themselves. They felt that with hard work people prospered and that position was significantly dependent on individual merit. Middle-class values of materialism, prosperity, and industriousness were dominant, and many Americans were middle-class people of modest fortunes. The people were sovereign and authority derived from the consent of the governed. The right to hold office was determined by majority vote and most men were free to compete for election. Where there was less equality than desired, free political institutions enabled the majority to seek to reduce inequality. If the higher classes dominated public office, gaining elective office depended on the ability to play to the common man and convince him that the office seeker could best represent him and his interests. All Americans were formally equal before the law. If America was far from perfectly egalitarian, as Tocqueville knew was true, America was also far less egalitarian than he claimed. At the same time, compared to aristocratic society Jacksonian America was indeed egalitarian.

Resulting partly from his underestimation of the existence of classes in America, Zeitlin (1971: 48-62) argues, Tocqueville also misses the importance of class conflict. Tocqueville does not deny the existence of classes (of a certain kind) or class conflict in America; however, viewing the American class structure in comparative-historical perspective, Tocqueville seeks to explain the moderate nature of that conflict.

Tocqueville holds that American politics can be analyzed in terms of the conflict basic to all free societies between those who, like the Federalists, wish to restrict popular power and those who, like the early Republicans, wish to extend it (1969: 174-179). The eventual supremacy of the Republicans (and later the Democrats) coupled with the demise of the Federalists symbolized the victory of egalitarianism over inegalitarianism. However, he sees the struggle continuing: "Aristocratic or democratic passions can easily be found at the bottom of all parties and . . . are . . . the nerve and soul of the matter" (1969: 178). And sometimes the forces of inequality win: Supported by the educated classes, the Bank of America withstands the combined assault of the president and the people (1969: 178). Defeated in the political arena, the wealthy have largely retired to private life, where they form their own society (1969: 179). Publicly pretending to be egalitarians, privately they disdain the people and democratic institutions and await the opportunity to reassert themselves politically (1969: 179). The temporary dominance of one group coupled with the political disintegration and withdrawal of the other moderates the divisiveness of the political expression of the class struggle.

Tocqueville also compared America to France, where class relations were marked by conflict, jealousy, and hatred, a heritage bequeathed to modern France by the old regime and the French Revolution. By comparison, American class conflict was moderate.

Marx identified the conditions transforming a class of itself into a genuine, politically organized, class-conscious class for itself; only the latter was an agent of social change. Classes in the United States, wrote Marx (1972: 444) in 1851-1852, were still fluid and there was great mobility between classes. Roughly thirty years later—half a century after Tocqueville's visit to America—Marx (1972: 333) emphasized the change in America. In the 1840s the proletarian movement was limited. However, by the 1880s large landowners were eliminating small and middle landowners, while in urban areas for the first time large capitalists and a mass proletariat grew together.

Within the constraints imposed by different perspectives, Marx's and Tocqueville's views of Jacksonian America are similar. In Marx's words, both analysts interpret the progressive elimination of "the *property qualification* for electors and representatives" as the victory of the masses "*over property owners and financial wealth*" (Marx, 1972: 31). Marx asserted the inevitability not of the democratic but of the proletarian revolution. Accordingly, he focused on what explained and foretold that revolution; but compared either to polarized capitalist society or America in the 1880s, Marx found unsolidified classes and low levels of class consciousness in Jacksonian America. Similarly, Tocqueville (1969: 430, 557) felt that although Americans may be divided into groups of rich, moderately well-to-do, and poor, genuine classes of rich, well-to-do, and poor did not exist. Living to see the change America underwent in the half century subsequent to Tocqueville's visit, Marx portrayed the America of the decades immediately preceding his own death quite differently from that described in *Democracy*. Nonetheless, neither Marx nor Tocqueville identified class conflict as the central dynamic of change in Jacksonian America. Rather, both saw America as a society with classes but not "genuine" "classes for themselves" and, consequently, moderate levels of class conflict.

Industrialization. In missing the impact of industrialization on the class structure, Tocqueville is held to have missed the way in which it spawned new classes and class relations, concentrated power in the hands of capitalists, and caused inequality, polarization, and class conflict. Lively (1962: 216-217) identifies "the growth of vast inequalities in the distribution of industrial wealth [and] the consolidation of highly articulated social classes welded into unity by class theories of economics and politics" as developments that "ill-fitted Tocqueville's picture of a democratic society."

Exemplifying his concern with political economy, Tocqueville describes how industrialization is fed by the materialistic demand for more and more goods found among democratic peoples. Mass markets attract the ambitious anxious to become successful manufacturers. Freed of the reciprocal bonds analogous to those linking aristocracy and peasantry in free aristocratic society, workers are dehumanized by coercive working conditions imposed by employers to extract as much work from them as possible. Expanding markets attract more and more manufacturers and competition promotes the growth of some as the more successful eliminate the less successful. Altogether, manufacturing employs ever greater numbers of increasingly alienated and debased workers.

During his second visit to England (in 1835) Tocqueville (1968a: 82-98) visited the industrial cities of Birmingham and Manchester, where much of what he saw repelled him. Permeated by the never-ceasing sounds of industry, Birmingham was an immense workplace where, dirtied by smoke, people struggled energetically to survive and prosper. However, his (1968a: 93) comparison of Birmingham and Manchester showed that, repulsive as it was, Birmingham was far from representing industrialization at its worst. In Manchester competition with workers from Ireland lowered the wages of the English workers to almost the same low level as that of the Irish. Whereas most Birmingham houses were each inhabited by a single family, in Manchester up to fifteen people lived crowded together in unhealthy, damp cellars. Polarization was far more extreme in Manchester, where there were a few great capitalists, a small middle class, and vast numbers of poor workers, two or three thousand of whom, many of them women or children, sometimes worked in a single factory. In Birmingham there were few large and many small industrialists and the workers, mostly men, worked at home or in small workshops with the owners themselves.

Tocqueville's (1968a: 92-98) visit to Manchester, where workers were caught "between poverty and death" (1968a: 95) stimulated his classic account of industrialization and polarization at their worst. The city showed the power of liberty freed of the necessary guidance of society and government. Everywhere the vast structures of industry clothed workers in smoke.

Here is the slave, there the master; there the wealth of some, here the poverty of most; there the organized effort of thousands produce, to the profit of one man, what society has not yet learnt to give. Here the weakness of the individual seems more feeble and helpless even than in the middle of a wilderness; here the effects, there the causes [1968a: 96].

The sun appeared as a rayless disk through the black industrial smoke covering the city. Preoccupied with their work, the ever hurrying people were as somber as their environment.

From this foul drain the greatest stream of human industry flows out to fertilise the whole world. From this filthy sewer pure gold flows. Here humanity attains its most complete development and its most brutish; here civilisation works its miracles, and civilised man is turned back almost into a savage [1968a: 96].

Underlying Tocqueville's analysis is the hope that just as France could profit from an understanding of democracy in America, so also industrializing France could profit from an understanding of more industrialized England, including her worst examples. Manufacturing threatened human dignity, rights, and freedom. Just as the tension between the demand for equality and the inequality perpetuated in the social structure helped cause the French Revolution, so the tension between employer-employee inequality and the general trend toward equality causes revolutionary tension. The growing concentration of the working class facilitates its collective action. In France,

equality increasingly extends its dominion everywhere—except in industry, which is moving in a more aristocratic direction every day. . . . Capital is concentrated in a few hands; the profits of those providing work is disproportionate to the worker's wage; the worker is in a position from which it is hard to escape, for he is situated at a great social distance from his employer, and is dependent on him.

Such shocking disparities cannot exist for too long in one society without producing a deep malaise [Tocqueville and Beaumont, 1968: 200].

Tocqueville predicted that the industrial class would be the source of revolutions not only in France but throughout the Western world. However far in the future they lay, such revolutions should cause concern, both because they reflect the deplorable condition of industrial workers and because, like all revolutions, they will be accompanied by the disorder and class hatred that undermine freedom.

Clearly, Tocqueville (1969: 685), who anticipates that the industrial class might become almost the only class in democratic society, does not slight industrialization. However, the importance he attaches to it varies, depending on the context. If he recognizes its importance, it is not the constant centerpiece of his analysis, the way freedom or equality is or to the degree that it is found in Marx's analysis of capitalism. Although a draft for *Democracy* asserts that "the progress of equality and the development of industry are the two great facts of our time" (quoted in Schleifer, 1980: 168), the published version relegates industrialization to a subordinate position.

Tocqueville's varying stress on the importance of industrialization should occasion little surprise. The degree to which modern society was agricultural-rural versus industrial-urban varied from country to country and over time. Jacksonian America was overwhelmingly rural; in 1830 only 3.2% of the population lived in cities of 50,000 or more. The corresponding figure for the United Kingdom is more than 400% higher (14.9%; Banks, 1971: 93, 95). Furthermore, there is the question of trends. For instance, by 1960, 36.1% of the American population lived in cities of 50,000 or more (Banks, 1971: 95). The more Tocqueville saw industrialization as like equality, that is, as the decisive trend of the future, the more he would be encouraged to emphasize it. The more he focused on contemporary society and the existing agricultural-rural versus industrial-urban balance, the less this would be so. Contemporary authors who evaluate Tocqueville in terms of those trends he "should" have foreseen honor his prescience, but the comparison between Jacksonian and post-Jacksonian America helps put Tocqueville's work and what he "should" have done in context.

Industrialization helped Tocqueville define types of society. For instance, he contrasts the agricultural American South with the industrial North. Modern industry had a decisively negative impact on the freedom and dignity of workers. Its society-wide influence was proportional to its extensiveness. In those societies Tocqueville studied he did not consider industry the decisive determinant of a nation's level of freedom. Rather than seek to explain a nation's overall level of freedom as a direct function of its level of industrialization, Tocqueville assesses its importance for those variables that he uses to explain freedom, particularly equality, the concentration of power, and community.

Tocqueville has been criticized for overestimating the egalitarianism of Jacksonian America and for underestimating the importance of industrialization as a cause of inequality and as a driving force of change in the modern world. Assessment of the empirical accuracy of his accounts is essential. Taking the empirically given level of equality and industrialization into account, the theoretical task is to assess his theory's utility in explaining freedom. However helpful critics have been in demonstrating greater inequality in America than Tocqueville saw and in reminding us of the importance of industrialization as a source of change and inequality, they have largely failed to show how the suggested empirical corrections of Tocqueville limit the validity of his theoretical propositions, the range of their applicability, or suggest correctives to strengthen his theory. Of course, Tocqueville himself asserts that concentrations of economic power and the vast inequality typically accompanying industrialization reduced freedom.

Focus on industrialization may be appropriate in assessing theories of the rise of the modern economic order or, because he seeks to explain social change as a function of changes in the way people materially produce, as articulated in class structure and class conflict, in Marx's theory of the transition from feudalism to capitalism and from capitalism to communism. Although Tocqueville is centrally concerned with change and states elements of a theory of revolution, his is not primarily a theory of social change. Tocqueville's theory is equally applicable to aristocratic and democratic society, to democracies with varying levels of equality, and to preindustrial, industrial, and post-industrial (Bell, 1976) society. Varying levels of equality or industrialization do not make the theory more or less applicable; rather, the impact of variation in each on the values of Tocqueville's key variables must be determined. Once this is done his theoretical assertions can be assessed. By *not* limiting it to societies with a given level of equality or economic structure and, as applied to democratic society, by not tying it too closely to industrialization, Tocqueville increases the range of societies to which his theory applies.

Tocqueville's Sympathies, Values, Ideology, and Prescriptions

None of the categories—conservative, liberal, radical—adequately defines Tocqueville. With conservatives he valued religion, order, respect for law, and diffused power. He held a limited view of what the state should attempt and regretted democracy's debasement of culture. Yet, he accepted the French Revolution insofar as it sought to promote liberty, fraternity, and equality; and he sought to convince conservatives that rather than futilely opposing modernity and attempting to reestablish the old order they must accept the democratic revolution and seek to give it the guidance necessary to realize its strengths and minimize its evils. With liberals he sought to promote the inherent rights and maximize the freedom of the individual. He was concerned about encroachments, especially by government, on individual autonomy and freedom. He believed that humans were endowed with sufficient intelligence to make them the best judge of their own interests and he considered them capable of shaping their own future. To this degree he was a nineteenth-century liberal. Yet, he rejected a society based on the individual pursuit of narrowly defined self-interest, and in France many liberals were anti-religious, whereas Tocqueville sought to combine freedom and religion. With radicals he endorsed equality, albeit far more equivocally than they did. Yet, in France radicals were often his greatest political foes. He rejected their attacks on religion, the means they advocated to realize their goals, and their faith in the state and the virtually unlimited possibilities of political power.

"I do not choose," Tocqueville (1862, 1: 381) wrote a friend, "to be confounded with those friends of order who are indifferent to freedom and justice, provided that they can sleep quietly in their beds." Rather, even while he maintained his unwavering commitment to liberty he hoped "to show so much respect for justice, such sincere love of order and law, such a deliberate attachment to morality and religion, that I cannot but believe that I shall be discovered to be a liberal of a new kind." Perhaps Tocqueville's self-designation as a liberal of a new kind is as appropriate as any.

Tocqueville had mixed feelings about both aristocracy and democracy. Aristocracies excel in foreign affairs, democracies in managing internal affairs: They promote public spirit, respect for law, internal resources, and prosperity (1969: 228-230; 1971: 77). He combined an "intellectual taste for democratic institutions" with aristocratic instincts, "which means that I scorn and fear the crowds" (quoted in Redier, 1925: 48).

If Tocqueville disliked the mediocrity and uniformity of democracy, the vulgarity of the masses, and the threat to law, order, and freedom posed by their unruly propensities, he also valued equality. Addressing the consequences of the transition from aristocracy to democracy, *Democracy's* conclusion (1969: 702-705) amplifies his feelings about equality. Democracy's leveling will reduce genius, perfection, and brilliance and the more exalted aristocratic virtues such as heroic devotion. Contemplating democracy's drab uniformity depresses Tocqueville and tempts him to regret the loss of what used to be. When inequality prevailed Tocqueville prefers to focus on the few great, wealthy, learned individuals, ignoring the vast majority who were poor, ignorant, and insignificant. However, Tocqueville feels that this selective perception results from a weakness not shared by God, whose view simultaneously encompasses each individual as well as all humanity and who desires not the exceptional prosperity of the few but the general well-being of all. "What seems to me decay is thus in His eyes progress. . . . Equality may be less elevated, but *it is more just, and in its justice lies its greatness and beauty"* (1969: 704; emphasis added). Accepting this divine plan, Tocqueville judged people, events, and institutions accordingly.

Tocqueville was powerfully drawn to the diversity and greatness of aristocratic society. At the same time, intellectually and emotionally he was a Christian. Christianity emphasized the equality of all people, asserted their natural rights, and taught them to love each other. Tocqueville endorsed democracy as the best guarantee of equal justice and the other basic human rights.

Weber (1958a: 120-121) distinguishes between an ethic of ultimate ends and an ethic of responsibility. The first orients behavior solely to ultimate ends; discounting responsibility for any evil consequences, actors attribute them not to their behavior but to human nature or the world. Though also oriented to ultimate ends, those employing an ethic of responsibility assume responsibility for the consequences of their behavior. They recognize that the attainment of good ends often requires the use of morally questionable means and that behavior motivated by the best of intentions may nonetheless have evil consequences.

Tocqueville employs the ethic of responsibility. His attitudes, behavior, and policy preferences were influenced by his own complex mix of values. As an outsider analyzing free societies experiencing orderly change, Tocqueville sounds like a democrat or even a radical. Writing as a friend of democracy, he (1969) finds much to admire in America which, despite its inherent shortcomings, in many ways exemplifies Tocqueville's image of modern democratic society at its best. Notwithstanding some basic similarities, Tocqueville (1968a: 72-74) notes four differences between English and French radicals: (1) Law abiding English radicals have no desire to impose on their fellow citizens policies contrary to their own choosing. Contemptuous of the law, French radicals attempt to use power to impose policies ensuring the happiness of the people (1968a: 73). (2) and (3) English radicals respect and French radicals attack religion and the rights of private property. (4) Although English radicals are well educated gentlemen knowledgeable about politics and history, French radicals are poor, boorish, ignorant about political science and much else, and preoccupied with the use of force. Tocqueville (1968a: 74) concludes that in England "an enlightened, man of good sense and good will would be a Radical."

Marx was a radical political outsider, whereas for just over a decade Tocqueville was an active and sometimes important participant in national French politics. We compare their stands on some proposed radical reforms designed to help the French poor. Marx emphasizes the alienation and degradation of the working class in capitalist society, shows how a free market and other bourgeoisie freedoms were used to mask and justify inequality, virtual slavery, and other injustice, advocates employment of the means, possibly including violence and revolution itself, necessary to transform capitalist into communist society, values the proletariat as the agent of this transformation, and asserts the potential of all humankind inherent in human nature. Vouching for the depth and authenticity of the poor's primary demand, the demand for equality, abhorring the conditions of the urban working class, and deploring the degradation of manufacturing, Tocqueville longs to rectify the plight of the poor. However, he finds it difficult to identify the necessary reforms. Though supporting the intent of radical reforms designed to help the working class and the destitute, Tocqueville concludes that, on balance, they would do more harm than good. His (Tocqueville and Beaumont, 1968: 1-27) 1835 "Memoir on Pauperism" delivered to the Royal Academic Society of Cherbourg asserts the importance of alleviating the wretchedness of the poor. Ideally, distinguishing between the deserving and undeserving poor, only the former would be helped. In practice, however, the distinction cannot be made. Making work the price of relief is also desirable but impractical. A given area will not always require enough public work, and the administrative difficulties in deciding what work is to be done at what pay as well as supervising it are overwhelming (Tocqueville and Beaumont, 1968: 15-16).

Tocqueville's "Memoir" also rejected extensive public as opposed to private charity. The need to live and the desire to improve one's living conditions counter the natural human tendency toward idleness. In destroying these incentives to work, the only ones sufficient to motivate most people, widespread availability of charity promotes idleness and the squandering of the income. Worse, officially certifying their inferiority, public charity stigmatizes people and thereby degrades them even more than it impoverishes them (Tocqueville and Beaumont, 1968: 17).

The English experience revealed some of the additional undesirable effects of public charity (Tocqueville and Beaumont, 1968: 19-20). Even as it reduced private charity it increased lower-class illegitimacy, indigency, and criminality. Furthermore, counties gave public charity only to their established residents. Thereby, in restricting the movement of those who receive it, public charity reduces the pauper's freedom.

Tocqueville (Tocqueville and Beaumont, 1968: 24-25) does advocate public charity to alleviate the inevitable problems associated with infancy, old age, sickness, insanity, and public disasters. He also supports free schools for the children of the poor. The labor of the working class supports the material well-being of the entire society (Tocqueville and Beaumont, 1968: 9). One consequence of an expansive public charity would be an indolent underclass living at the expense of the working class (Tocqueville and Beaumont, 1968: 17). These considerations lead Tocqueville to conclude that even if some public charity is advisable, on balance, it actually harms the working class. Given the increasing needs generated by the growth of the industrial classes, Tocqueville (Tocqueville and Beaumont, 1968: 26-27) acknowledged the inadequacy of private charity, even though it is a good thing in itself and preferable to public charity. Asserting the existence of alternatives to public charity as a means of reducing pauperism, Tocqueville (Tocqueville and Beaumont, 1968: 26-27) promised to treat the topic in a later work which, however, he apparently never wrote (Tocqueville and Beaumont, 1968: 27n).

Thirteen years later Tocqueville's (Tocqueville and Beaumont, 1968: 179-192) "Speech on the Right to Work" to the French Chamber of Deputies identifies two consequences of a proposed constitutional amendment that would grant to everyone the absolute right to work. First, the state might become the principal or even the only industrial entrepreneur, turning taxation from the means of running the government into the chief means of supporting industry. Tocqueville also opposes the elimination of private property. Second, the state might find jobs in industry for workers, but then, as the sole organizer of labor, the state would be led to regimenting industry. Either consequence of the state's guaranteeing the right to work would lead to the centralization of administration and monolithic state control that Tocqueville despises.

Beyond his negative assessments of the specific policies advocated by champions of the poor and the working class, Tocqueville dislikes the party with the closest links to the working class, the socialist. He (Tocqueville and Beaumont, 1968: 182-83) rejects each of what he sees as the three principal traits of socialism. First, encouraging people's concern for their material well-being, socialism increases and promises to fulfill their materialistic aspirations. Both symbolizing and strengthening the characteristic malaise of the democratic age, socialism is a part of the problem, not the solution. Second, socialism attacks private property, which Tocqueville feels is virtually coterminous with organized society. Viewing it as an invaluable source of people's economic power and independence, Tocqueville applauds the French Revolution's role in distributing it more evenly and wishes to see such widespread distribution perpetuated. Third, socialism scorns, distrusts, or undermines much of what Tocqueville most values: liberty, human reason, and respect for the individual. Contrary to his belief that individuals are the best judge of their own self-interest and should be accorded the greatest possible freedom, socialism wishes to control and mold them.

Representing the contemporary form of the servitude of the old regime, Tocqueville sees socialism as contrary to the enduring, authentic goals of the French Revolution (Tocqueville and Beaumont, 1968: 183-186). Whereas the Revolution achieved greatness by appealing to higher feelings, socialism appeals to base, materialistic desires. Whereas the Revolution respected the sacredness of private property and consequently distributed it more widely, socialism attacks it. Whereas the Revolution, fought in the name of liberty, broke the shackles of the old regime and thereby restored individuality, assuming responsibility for everything, socialism negates individuality and independence. Socialism and the French Revolution are alike in one way—both sought equality; but whereas the Revolution sought equality in freedom, socialism seeks it in servitude.

Tocqueville (1970: 102) recognizes that his class origins play a part in his condemnation of socialism. He finds it easier to associate with fellow aristocrats whose political views differ from his than with politicians and officials of middle- or lower-class origins who hold similar views. If Tocqueville (1970: 102) dislikes the boorishness of socialism's leaders, he has deeper reasons for rejecting them and their ideology. The socialists advocate violent, revolutionary means that Tocqueville feels promote the disorder, disrespect for law, and unruliness favorable to tyranny. Revolutions promote centralization and create a legacy of class hatred that undermines the community necessary for freedom. The product of diseased imaginations (1872, 1: 36), socialist theories promulgated doctrines contrary to "the unalterable laws that constitute society itself" (1970: 75). No good but only anger, disorder, and unhealthy conflict could result from the way socialism created expectations inherently impossible to fulfill. Promising to free workers "from the necessities of their condition," socialism instead promised them an "imaginary well-being . . . as a right" (1970: 136). It contained

> chimerical ideas on the relations between labour and capital, extravagant theories as to the degree in which the Government might interfere between the working man and the employer, doctrines of ultra-centralisation which had at last persuaded large numbers that it depended on the State not only to save them from want but to place them in easy comfortable circumstances [1872, 1: 35-36].

In their democratic-revolutionary tenor, attacks on privilege and diversity, love of equality, lack of concern for private rights, contempt for the past, dislike of secondary institutions, local powers, and other sources of local freedom and checks on the power of the state, boundless faith in intellectual panaceas, and faith in an all-powerful state as the mechanism of reform, the Economists (Physiocrats) were the old regime's proponents of that democratic despotism to which contemporary socialists are the ideological heirs (1955: 158-165). Socialism's goal—an all-powerful state restructuring society to ensure uniformity and equality in servitude—was anathema to Tocqueville.

Rejecting socialism, Tocqueville (Tocqueville and Beaumont, 1968: 174-178) drafted a manifesto (published posthumously) specifying how legislation should seek to help the lower social orders: give them political rights, involve them in politics, improve both their intellectual and material conditions, and give them all the legal equality compatible with private property and the inequality that flows from it.

Marx often defines capitalist and communist society as polar opposites: one embodied inequality, class conflict, contradiction, irrationality, injustice, slavery, alienation, and the degrading distortion of human nature; the other equality, harmony, community, rationality, justice, human realization, and freedom. Viewing capitalism as progressive in many ways, Marx lauds its productivity and analyzes it as the evolutionary stage (sometimes treating it as the necessary evolutionary state) preceding communism. However, in contrasting capitalism with its irrational production for profit and communism with its unfettered, rational production for human needs, he sees the one as good, the other as bad. Tocqueville also defines societies as polar opposites: Aristocracy is defined by inequality, democracy by equality. He (for example, 1969: 14-15, 229-235; especially p. 245) does not evaluate these historical stages as moral opposites, however. Each is seen as a mixture of strengths and weaknesses and either could be good (free) or bad (despotic). Tocqueville himself was less concerned to choose between them than he was to encourage people to recognize the inevitability of the democratic revolution and focus their efforts on making democracy free.

Just as numerous elements in Marx converge to make him a wholehearted champion of the working class, a complex mixture of elements in Tocqueville leave him only an equivocal champion. A utopian thinker with a highly optimistic image of human nature, Marx seeks societal shortcomings neither in it nor in the inherent nature of social life but in changeable aspects of social structures. In contrast, Tocqueville (Tocqueville and Beaumont, 1968: 16) warns against such utopian thinking: "Laws must be made for men and not in terms of a perfect world which cannot be sustained by human nature, nor of models which it offers only very occasionally." Reflecting his view of human nature, and, perhaps, attributing virtues to them, which they lacked, Marx sees the proletariat as the instrument that would usher in utopian society. Of aristocratic background and holding a less optimistic view of human nature, Tocqueville is hardly prone to over-estimating the virtues of the working class (however, see 1872, 1: 38). Marx (1972: 352-53) forecast the class (political) rule of the proletariat as a transitory stage preceding communism. "In place of the old bourgeois society, with its classes and class antagonisms, we shall have an association, in which the free development of each is the condition for the free development of all" (1972: 353). Tocqueville, like the authors of the Federalist Papers, fears all unbalanced concentrations of power. Viewing control over the means of production as the decisive form of power and treating conflict over these means as the basic conflict that structures and from which other conflicts are ultimately derivative, Marx believes that once everyone shared the same relationship to the means of production as a result of common ownership, classes and the structural basis of conflict would disappear. The state as the reflection of the interests of one class and as the instrument of its rule, or, more generally, of one part of society against another, would be abolished. Marx expects this transcendence of the distinction between state and civil society to be achieved through "universal suffrage, whose effective existence implies the dialectical overcoming and disappearance of the state as a distinct organism" (Avineri, 1968: 210). With or without common ownership of the means of production, Tocqueville envisions no transcendence of the state, no elimination of the distinction between civil and political society, and no elimination of social conflict. There are many sources of such conflict other than those derived from a differential relationship to the means of production. Far from volun-tarily giving it up, the politically powerful and governments themselves seek to increase their power. Regardless of state claims to represent the common interests of all, unless effectively checked those with power are likely to use it to further their own interests and there will always be conflict over control of the state itself. Indeed, Tocqueville anticipates that any increased power resulting from increased control over the means of production would intensify conflict over control of the state. Believing that, depending on specific historical circumstances, prole-tarian revolution might be a historical necessity and believing also in the inevitability of utopian communism, Marx endorses conflict and sometimes even violent revolution as the agent and price of progress. Recognizing that conflict is inherent in social life, Tocqueville feels that beyond a certain level it threatens the things he values most. Marx sees no reason to reject even radical reforms designed to help the working class and the poor. Insofar as such reforms might fall short or have some undesirable effects, these simply reflect the inherent defects of capitalist society and constitute just so many additional demonstrations of the necessity of transforming capitalism into communism. Tocqueville rejects many radical reforms designed to help the poor as more harmful than beneficial. Marx, a radical utopian thinker, champions the poor and especially the working class in a way that Tocqueville, a realistic liberal thinker, could not.

Tocqueville faced a dilemma. His morality mandated that all people be treated with human dignity and guaranteed equal justice and human rights. Recognizing that vast inequality inevitably results in differential power and unequal justice, he endorsed the trend toward equality and felt that modern society must keep inequality within reasonable bounds. His political program for France included as goals legal and political equality and improvement of the intellectual and material conditions of the lower classes. Yet, he rejects the programs advocated by socialists and other radicals designed to achieve these ends; and measured against the inequality of French society and his own goals, his practical suggestions for reform are modest (for example, 1862, 2: 85-87; see also Drescher, 1964a: 125-151). He can also sound harsh and conservative. In a private conversation with Ampere and his English friend Senior, Tocqueville (1872, 1: 204-205) questioned whether or not the law should ensure that no one would starve. "If we give this right we must of course make this relief disagreeable; we must separate families, make the workhouse a prison, and our charity repulsive."

We may speculate that in some measure Tocqueville was locked into the contours of the existing political dialogue. Certain reforms might have brought about desired goals without the undesirable consequences he attributed to the radical reforms he rejected, for example, public charity or the right to work. For instance, sufficiently progressive taxes on income, property, and wealth could produce a more egalitarian distribution of society's material goods. Use of tax revenues to promote a strong educational system available to students regardless of their financial resources would distribute opportunity more widely. Such programs could respect private property and, indeed, like the French Revolution, by distributing it more widely, spread a resource that Tocqueville viewed as a source of individual freedom. These and other reforms could respect private property and individual rights, spread opportunity, and promote and reward individual industriousness without massive centralization and governmental control of the individual.

Perhaps Tocqueville places too much emphasis on his concern for order and too frequently subordinates the implications of his own understanding that, in Tawney's words, "freedom for the pike is death for the minnows" (Tawney as quoted in Lively, 1962: 220). Perhaps he gives insufficient weight to the way in which the inequality associated with poverty and exploitation of the lower classes denies justice and freedom. Perhaps he suffers a failure of imagination or of will in not identifying and forcefully promoting measures that, while avoiding the defects of those radical reforms he rejects, would remedy the evils that so trouble him. With hindsight and from the vantage point of modern, liberal, democratic society, Tocqueville could be criticized for failing to be a stronger champion of the exploited and the poor and not being truer to some of his own values. However, final assessment of Tocqueville should also give careful attention to his *Recollections* (1970), personal correspondence and conversations (for example, 1862, 1872), which provide moving accounts of a principled politician who, guided by an ethic of responsibility, struggled to realize his values in an imperfect world. (For one account see Gargan, 1955.)

Approaches to Tocqueville and Marx

Given their differences it is not surprising that the usual approach to Marx and Tocqueville is to oppose and then choose between them. For analyses of modern (capitalist) society the selection is often made on the basis of Marx's emphasis on inequality versus Tocqueville's on equality. A Marxist might identify the economic bases of inequality in capitalist society and then apply Marxian perspectives to identify the causes and consequences of these inequalities. A Tocquevillian (assuming one exists!) addressing modern society might use Tocqueville to analyze equality. For instance, acknowledging that America is far from being perfectly egalitarian, Dahl (1976; especially pp. 54-55, 96-119, 255-257) uses Tocqueville as a theoretical resource in his account of egalitarianism in America. Or theorists, followers of neither Marx nor Tocqueville, may choose between the two, depending on their assessment of the inequality in the period to be analyzed. Warner (1976: 37-49) feels Tocqueville is useful for understanding the contrast between aristocratic and democratic society and for analyzing early and Jacksonian America. Although Tocqueville "provides a profound analysis of the effects of egalitarianism," he did not understand the impact that concentrated wealth would have on the development of democratic society. "For an understanding of modern social structure as deriving from resurgent economic inequalities, the works of Karl Marx provide a more compelling insight" (Warner, 1976: 49).

Without denying the important differences between them or that one may be preferable to the other, depending on the trends or social structure to be analyzed and the question posed, I suggest that it is often fruitful to treat them in a more complementary way. The emphases of each theorist can be used to check, correct, or supplement those of the other. Rather than taking either the trend toward equality or inequality as basic and explaining away the other, I suggest taking both trends seriously and assessing their complex interactions. To use America as an example, industrialization and the market have been sources of inequality and the concentration of power. An equally important aspect of American history has been the struggles accompanying the partially successful claims for equality of different groups—non-property holders, blacks, women, Hispanics, homosexuals, the disabled, the elderly, and other minorities. Legislation providing floors for all citizens, spreading rights and entitlements, and mitigating market and other inequalities has been proposed, debated, rejected, passed, and once passed, sometimes rolled back. If Marx forces us to come to grips with greater inequality in American society than Tocqueville foresaw, Tocqueville helps us understand America's egalitarian ethos and the dominance of the middle class; why society has not polarized the way Marx predicted; why, far from having undergone a revolutionary transformation into communism, America has instead remained relatively stable and anti-revolutionary; and why America has experienced mild oscillations around a center that has moved slowly to the left. More generally, because each theorist identifies and explains basic aspects of modern society, complementary use of their perspectives seems a more promising approach than does opposing and choosing between them.

DURKHEIM

Durkheim and Tocqueville produce an odd contrast—their similarities are as striking as their differences. By emphasizing either, they can be portrayed as different or alike. Collins (1968) contrasts Tocqueville and Weber with such systems theorists as Marx, and, most particularly, Durkheim and Parsons. Assuming an underlying continuity in their thought, Turner and Beeghley (1981: 330-333; 324-328) treat Tocqueville in terms of his influence on Durkheim.

Image of Society

Durkheim employs different images of society. Rather than carefully distinguishing them, he shifts back and forth among a number of more or less clearly delineated, partially overlapping images, making it difficult if not impossible to offer any single formal definition of what he means by "society." If he thinks of society as composed of individuals organized into groups, his other conceptions are more distinctive.

Durkheim was an evolutionary structural-functionalist. He often employed biological analogies and likened society to biological organisms, particularly humans. The overall course of social change is the evolution of society from a simple, structurally homogeneous society integrated by mechanical solidarity—of which the collective conscience is the proximate source and that is based on the mutual attractiveness produced by likeness—into a complex, differentiated society integrated not only by a moral solidarity similar to mechanical solidarity but also by the organic solidarity based on the mutual attraction of differentiated, specialized, mutually dependent parts (Durkheim, 1960). Viewing society as a structural-functional system, he analyzes its parts in terms of their contribution to society and its evolutionary development. I cite as examples basic institutions analyzed at length in some of his books: education socializes and prepares the child for adult life (Durkheim, 1956, 1961); "the very organ of social thought" whose "principal function is to think," the state, locus of the highest "degree of consciousness and reflection," makes decisions for the society (Durkheim, 1958: 50-51); the division of labor is the basic source of solidarity in modern society (Durkheim, 1960); and religion integrates society (Durkheim, 1965).

A third Durkheimian image is that of substratum and superstructure. He refers to the substratum as the morphological or anatomical structure of society, that is, the spatial distribution and grouping of people and the lines of communication and transportation linking them. This is an image of society as something whose structure can be mapped. This morphological structure is crucial because of its influence on interaction, which generates the superstructure, for example, consciousness, moral rules, and institutions.

Durkheim emphasized the moral-symbolic nature of social reality. He held an increasingly idealist conception of society as a psychic phenomenon. This conception can be seen as an outgrowth of his third image or as sufficiently distinct to constitute a fourth image of society. This fourth image views the collective conscience (*The Division of Labor in Society*; hereafter referred to as *Division*), collective sentiments (*Suicide*), or collective representations (*The Elementary Forms of the Religious Life*; hereafter referred to as *The Elementary Forms*) as the core of society. If Durkheim continued to consider the base an integral part of society and to assert its influence on collective representations, he also increasingly came to assert the partial autonomy of collective representations "which, once born, obey laws all their own," (Durkheim, 1965: 471), their importance, and to see them as the essence of society. Sociology is "a form of psychology," namely, "collective psychology" (Durkheim, quoted in Lukes, 1972: 234n;

Durkheim, 1974: 34n). Society is ultimately composed of collective representations. In the social realm "more than anywhere else, the idea is the reality" (Durkheim, 1965: 260) and society "above all is the idea which it forms of itself" (Durkheim, 1965: 470). It manifests the most rational form of intellectual and psychic life (Durkheim, 1965: 28-29, 466, 470, 483, 490, 492-493). In sum, society "is the highest form of the psychic life, since it is the consciousness of the consciousnesses" (Durkheim, 1965: 492).

Force Imagery

Durkheim's force imagery is as central to his sociology as it is widely overlooked (Takla and Pope, 1985). He (1965: 233) feels that all "the world is a system of forces" and conceptualizes social phenomena accordingly. Their nature as forces makes social phenomena appropriate objects of scientific study; embodying force, social phenomena are causes that produce determinate effects.

Permeating his sociology generally, Durkheim's force imagery helps define a basic dichotomy, that between the social and the individual (Durkheim, 1973b). As forces, their relations are complex: interpenetration, interdependence, and mutual reinforcement, on the one hand, and inherent antagonism and mutual enervation, on the other. Neither the individual nor society can exist without the other. Empirically, society presupposes the individuals who constitute it and without whom and whose thought it cannot exist (Durkheim, 1965: 240, 253, 387-389, 471). Through their normal functioning social forces, like all natural forces, lose strength (Durkheim, 1965: 379, 387-390). Without periodic rejuvenation, society languishes and dies (Durkheim, 1965: 263, 387, 465-466). At the same time "man is man," because of his social existence and cultural heritage (Durkheim, 1965: 29, 243, 357, 388-389). Just as social forces are expended, so also the strength of individuals withers, as they pursue their everyday, utilitarian lives. They are thus dependent on contact with social, collective realities to give them the renewed energy necessary to pursue life (Durkheim, 1965: 240, 257, 390-392, 427, 464). Notwithstanding these relationships of interpenetration and mutual dependence, society and the individual are not only analytically distinct—neither can be reduced to the other (Durkheim, 1965: 28-29, 237, 289, 388-389, 471)—but are opposed (Durkheim, 1965: 237, 297-299, 307, 351, 355-358, 390, 494), antagonistic (Durkheim, 1965: 256-257; Durkheim, 1951: 319; see also Durkheim, 1960: 130, 92) forces.

Similarities and Differences

Although Tocqueville also portrays society as composed of individuals arranged in more and less organized groups, he does not employ the more distinctively Durkheimian images of society and is not an evolutionary structural-functionalist. He does not define society as a system, does not employ a society-biological organism analogy, and does not turn to Darwinian or other evolutionary or biological theories as a resource for social theory.

Social Change. For Durkheim social phenomena are created through association. Their forms of association or the morphological structure of society (Durkheim, 1964: 112) determines society's internal environment or social milieu, which itself is "the determining factor of collective evolution" (Durkheim, 1964: 116; see also p. 113). Durkheim also postulates a one-to-one relationship between cause and effect: each cause has one and only one effect (Durkheim, 1951: 146), and each effect has one and only one cause (Durkheim, 1964: 128). Together these ideas help structure Durkheim's theory of social change, which postulates the same basic evolutionary trajectory for all societies. *Division* (Durkheim, 1960: 256-282, especially p. 266-275) identifies one basic cause, the struggle for existence, pushing societies along the evolutionary continuum from the simple to the complex.

Durkheim's basically unicausal theory of change (however, see also Durkheim, 1960: 283-328 and 1965: 471) applies to all societies, covers social evolution from earliest times to modern society, and, asserting a unilinear course of change with offshoots—like a tree with its main trunk and branches—postulates parallel and converging trajectories. Identifying "rules for distinguishing between the normal and the pathological," *The Rules* (Durkheim, 1964: 47-75) argues that what is widespread in a given type of society (species) is normal for that society. On the basis of this and other considerations, for example, institutions are functional, the theory identifies an expected course of change. Supporting empirical instances are considered normal, whereas the theoretically unexpected, defined as pathological, is treated as a function of exceptional, abnormal characteristics (Durkheim, 1960: 353-395; 1964: 47-75), thereby protecting the theory from falsification. As illustrated by his analysis of modern society, Durkheim's approach produces anomalies. Contrary to the criteria of normality identified in *The Rules, Division* (1960: 353-395) treats widespread forms of the division of labor, for example, the anomic and the forced division of labor, not as normal but as abnormal. Again, *Division* (1960: 353-395), unable to cite empirical examples of what is asserted to be the normal case, instead treats as abnormal such empirically widespread phenomena in capitalist society as industrial and commercial crises, conflict between capital and labor and among classes, and the injustice in the lack of correspondence between ability and reward.

Tocqueville's approach differs. He attributes change to internal, external, general, specific, accidental, and chance factors. Interacting in complex, partially indeterminate and partially unexpected ways, these factors are as capable of explaining converging or parallel as diverging developmental paths. Tocqueville empirically assesses societal change and then seeks to explain it. He does not use his theory to assert a theoretically expected course of change that departs from empirically given change. Accordingly, he is forced neither to confront deviations from theoretically projected change nor to resort to a normal-pathological distinction to explain such deviations.

Tocqueville's general views on change in history and society are, like Durkheim's, generally applicable. However, Tocqueville focuses on the transition from aristocracy to democracy in Western Europe, where his perspectives again contrast with Durkheim's. Durkheim (for example, 1973a) sees modern societies converging as free, just societies that value and promote individualism. Tocqueville analyzes them as complex mixtures of similarities produced by the democratic revolution and differences due to variations in freedom and the variables explaining it and due to each nation's idiosyncratic features such as its history, age, geographic location, national character, and culture. By emphasizing either similarities or differences an analyst employing Tocqueville's perspectives could argue that modern nations are similar or dissimilar. If Tocqueville emphasizes democratic commonalities and shows how, notwithstanding other differences, nations are governed by the relationships identified in his theory of freedom, he is equally sensitive to how their differences make each nation a unique historical phenomenon.

Tocqueville's perspective comes closest to Durkheim's in postulating a single continuum as the measure of modernity, but even here differences remain. Durkheim's continuum is structural-functional differentiation, Tocqueville's inequality-equality. Employing their respective continua, the two theorists develop different interpretations of Western European history. Durkheim pictures these nations as following similar developmental paths, as each becomes increasingly differentiated and integrated by organic solidarity. From their similar starting points in the Middle Ages Tocqueville (1955: 14-19) feels that they followed different developmental paths, most important, England that of freedom, France that of tyranny.

For Durkheim society is normally a tightly integrated system the parts of which mutually determine one another and the morphological structure of which is the ultimate causal determinant. Given their systemic nature, societies can be classified into evolutionarily distinct types or species (Durkheim, 1964: 76-88). Tocqueville sees only certain aspects of society as being bound together in mutually determinant ways. For example, equality interacts with the other aspects of society, is a cause, and there is some affinity between it and tyranny. Nonetheless, for Tocqueville the most important aspects of society, such as community and freedom, vary independently of the level of equality (Figure 3, Chapter 2). In contrast, Durkheim (1960) sees the most important aspects of modern society as linked to and determined by the amount of structural-functional differentiation and the relative strength of organic solidarity. In sum, Durkheim developed a general model that identifies and explains similarities in the conditions, causes, sequence, and consequences of change. Tocqueville's perspective asserts the importance of both similarities and differences, some of which lend themselves to generalization, some of which do not.

Though recognizing that not all institutions are functional, Durkheim explains why most are. The social institutions found throughout a particular social species must be the most advantageous, because otherwise their widespread existence would be incomprehensible (1964: 58). *The Rules* (1964: 97) offers a logical argument: Institutions can be maintained only at some cost. Therefore, most institutions must be beneficial because, if "the majority of social phenomena" were parasitic in character, "the budget of the organism would have a deficit and social life would be impossible."

Rejecting evolutionary structural-functionalism, Tocqueville has no need to explain why most institutions are functional. To the contrary, he recognizes that institutions that help perpetuate society and that are functional for some groups are dysfunctional for others. Feudal institutions perpetuated society and were advantageous to lords and, though benefiting peasants in some ways, also inflicted great hardships on them. Tocqueville condemns many institutions, for example, centralization of administration, as massively dysfunctional. Furthermore, he does not need to explain why their very functionality perpetuates institutions. He feels that a variety of interacting factors, important among which is the ability of powerful groups to perpetuate institutions advantageous to themselves, explain why institutions do and do not survive. Rather than employing the classic functionalist argument that explains existence by appeal to necessity, Tocqueville, sensitive to the arbitrary nature of social institutions, rejects such arguments. Indeed, would not functionalists have been spared many of their errors and modern sociology the ultimately tedious debate over functionalism (Demerath and Peterson, 1967) if sociologists had heeded his (1970: 76) more than century-old observation: "What are called necessary institutions are only institutions to which one is accustomed. . . . In matters of social constitution the field of possibilities is much wider than people living within each society imagine." Tocqueville's reminder is equally apropos as a warning against justifying institutions by appeals to inevitabilities or necessities, whether posed in the name of evolutionary or historicist appeals to region, race, class, religion, national destiny, or whatever.

This comparison of Tocqueville and Durkheim provides no grounds for asserting Tocqueville's influence on Durkheim's theory of social change. To the contrary, Durkheim's theory was formulated in the face of Tocqueville's rejection of absolute systems that link history by great first causes and thereby succeed in banishing people from the history of the human race (Tocqueville, 1970: 62; compare Durkheim, 1964: 89-124; Durkheim, 1960: 273).

Social Realism. Durkheim's idealist conception of society as a psychic phenomenon—as collective representations, collective sentiments, collective conscience, and collective consciousness—intersects his functionalism. Focusing on whether Durkheim commits the group-mind fallacy, commentators have typically overlooked the way in which his idealist conception of society helped him resolve a troublesome problem, namely, the link between necessity and existence. For Durkheim society is a sentient, conscious, rational entity that understands the conditions of its own existence. Society is also "the most powerful combination of physical and moral forces of which nature offers us an example" (Durkheim, 1965: 495). This combination of power and self-consciousness explains how and why society uses its power to compel individuals to engage in the collective religious rituals through which it is created, recreated, maintained, strenthened, and sometimes changed (Durkheim, 1965: 29, 391, 411, 466, 470, 474-475, 483, 490-495; 1961: 86).

Even beyond its functionalist components, there is much in Durkheim's image of society and approach to sociological explanation to which Tocqueville would object. Because for Tocqueville only individuals think, he would reject Durkheim's reification. Nor does Tocqueville share Durkheim's positivistic conception of social and historical phenomena as forces.

As a pioneer Durkheim was concerned to establish sociology as a science. Science is the study of reality, and each scientific discipline studies its own distinct reality. Sociology would legitimate itself as a science to the degree that it identified and demonstrated the importance of its own subject matter. All nature is inherently broken down into distinct levels or orders and the interaction or association of phenomena at each level creates emergent phenomena at the next higher level. *Suicide* (1951: 325n) orders these levels as follows: physical, chemical, biological, psychological, and sociological. Each level is a distinct reality to the degree that its forces are powerful and emergent. Forces are emergent to the degree that they embody power at a given level of reality and are not the product of and hence explained by forces at some other level of reality. These considerations underlie Durkheim's social realism; because social phenomena are powerful and emergent, they must be explained in terms of social causes.

Working within what he considers an established tradition of history, social science, and moral philosophy dating back at least to the ancient Greek philosophers, Tocqueville feels no need to establish a new science. Both men often employ a distinctively sociological approach which, for instance, generally rejects racial and other biological explanations of variation in human behavior and institutions. However, their road to the rejection of biological explanation of social phenomena differs. Durkheim's approach is based on a firm methodological rejction of such explanations (Durkheim, 1964: 89-124) reinforced by empirical and theoretical considerations (for example, Durkheim, 1951: 82-93). Tocqueville's is based both on moral considerations (the effect of such arguments is to degrade rather than elevate people) and on his assessment of the empirical and theoretical validity of such arguments, not on methodological commitment to the emergent nature of social realities.[2]

If there is something in Tocqueville comparable to Durkheim's concern to establish a separate discipline, perhaps it is his concern to be original. In preparing to write about a given topic he (1862, 2: 311, 323) tried to avoid reading other general interpretive-explanatory accounts, lest they influence his thinking and reduce his originality.[3] Apart from

---

2. Ironically, notwithstanding Durkheim's social realism, *Suicide* (1951: 215-216, 270-272, 385-386; see also Durkheim, 1960: 133-135) appeals to biologically given sexual differences to explain male-female differences in suicide. Tocqueville often entertains the possibility that biological differences explain some variation in human behavior; it is when biological explanations deny human freedom or are used to support doctrines that are degrading that Tocqueville forcefully rejects them. See Chapter 2.

3. Just how successful Tocqueville was in this quest to avoid being influenced by others must be assessed on a case-by-case basis. Where possible, he often sought the views of those being investigated. As his own notebooks reveal, many of the explanations in *Democracy* are largely identical to those of his informants or in the works he read about America (Tocqueville, 1971; see also Pierson, 1938; Schleifer, 1980), and Tocqueville's often flattering account of America overlaps with the Americans'

his concern to promote certain values, Tocqueville saw no need to legitimate his own work other than through making an original contribution. Like Tocqueville, Durkheim was concerned that his sociology have useful practical application and promote values that, unlike Tocqueville, he felt should be scientifically established. Tocqueville sought explanatory help wherever he could find it. Rather than seeking to establish an academic discipline, his work ranged across and synthesized explanations from what today is history, sociology, and both the empirical and normative traditions within political science.

Durkheim's social realism does not lead him to ignore individual social psychology. *Suicide's* social psychological analysis links social causes, specifically varying levels of integration and regulation, to variation in social suicide rates. For instance, Durkheim (1951: 212-214) argues that absence of meaning in life creates the depression that causes individuals to commit egoistic suicide. As the "prolongations" of social causes "inside of individuals" (Durkheim, 1951: 287), however, such social psychological states must always be understood as the effects of social causes. For Tocqueville social structural and social psychological causes exist in a state of partial mutual autonomy but also in a state of reciprocal influence. Their mutual relations vary from congruence and reinforcement to tension. The social psychology of democratic peoples perpetuates American institutions, whereas in France it helped cause the French Revolution. Although Durkheim's social realism eschews appeal to social psychological variables as causes of social phenomena, Tocqueville freely identified such phenomena as causes.

Both Durkheim and Tocqueville are centrally concerned with social power. For Durkheim social power is the force of society itself. The key variable attributes of forces are strength and direction (relative to other forces). Among the individual-society relations postulated by Durkheim is that of the individual and society as opposing forces. Viewing them in this way, his interest centers on their relative strength. He treats the absolute strength of the individual as a constant, making the relative strength of these opposing forces a function of the variable strength of social forces. The stronger social forces are the greater their strength as social causes, the greater their effects, the stronger moral rules and collective representations, the greater social control, the more integrated and orderly society, the more individuals and their behavior are a product of social forces, the greater altruism and conformity, the more individuals act in the service of social interests, the weaker egoism, and

---

own conventional wisdom about their culture, institutions, and national character. However, just as Marx's work is more than German philosophy, French socialism, and English economics. *Democracy* is more than the explanations found in the works read by Tocqueville or given him by innumerable Americans (and others).

the less frequent deviance. Durkheim has good reason to be concerned with the strength of social forces.

If Durkheim's (1973b) conception of the dualism of human nature, basic to which is his view of the unsocialized and unsocializable individual as a force opposed to social forces, directs attention to the relative strength of individual and social forces, his functionalism seeks to explain how society does what it must do to survive. Consistent with his functionalism, which approaches structures in terms of their contribution to society, Durkheim does not analyze the state as an instrument enabling some people to dominate others. He does view it, and, indeed, any viable group or institution, as a mechanism of social control, but this is seen as the functionally necessary control, not of one group over another, but rather of one part of society acting in the name and interest of society itself.

Durkheim's approach deflects attention from the struggle for power and the way in which the usual outcome of that struggle, the differential distribution of power, permits some groups to exploit others. His approach also defines the exploitative use of power and the ensuing conflict as abnormal. In the homogeneous primitive setting Durkheim analyzes the relationship between the individual and society, not how some individuals use their power to control others. Where a group in modern society uses its power to exploit another group and thereby violates the norms of modern justice or where the distribution of power and its exploitative use produce high levels of conflict, Durkheim (1960: 353-395) explains these not as expected outcomes but rather as products of the abnormal division of labor. He then seeks to show that in time these pathological developments will pass: Class conflict will abate; greater equality of opportunity will produce a more equitable relationship among ability, contribution, and reward; justice will prevail, and the different parts of society will make their necessary functional contributions. Society itself will do a better job of doing those things it must in order to progress, will increasingly realize its own high ideals, and will become healthy, integrated, and normal. Durkheim, then, approaches power as society's power to control the individual and do what it must to perpetuate itself.

Tocqueville does not think of the individual and society as opposing forces nor of social power as the power of society, conceived of as an emergent, reified phenomenon, over the individual. Rather, he views power as something that some people wield over others. He does not employ a normal-pathological distinction to explain away power's "dysfunctions" nor does he seek to show that normal evolutionary development would make power functional. Rather, he believes that the undesirable concentration and use of power, as in France, were as likely as its opposite configuration and use, as in England and the United States. Accordingly, his theory specifies the conditions of the desirable versus the undesirable distribution and use of power.

Integration and Anomie. Durkheim's is a theory of social integration. If he addresses social change, particularly changes in the causes and consequences of social integration, he is concerned to identify the appropriate bases of integration in modern society. Like Tocqueville, Durkheim is also greatly concerned with freedom. He seeks to demonstrate how in modern society freedom and individuality may be combined with integration. And like Durkheim, Tocqueville is vitally concerned with integration (community). If Durkheim's primary focus differs from Tocqueville's, their concerns also overlap; and although some of their analyses differ, given the important differences that separate them, others are surprisingly similar.

Both men are vitally concerned with solidarity, not least because of its links to morality. Embodying social power, emergent social phenomena for Durkheim are simultaneously the source of solidarity, order, and morality. Whereas primitive societies are integrated mechanically, modern societies are integrated organically (Durkheim, 1960). In primitive society there is one common (collective) conscience, in organic society a collective conscience for each group in the society, plus that common to the entire society. In addition, the content of the collective conscience differs. In primitive society it is more concrete, embodies repressive law that imposes severe sanctions for moral infractions, and stresses the values and interests of the group at the expense of those of the individual. In modern society the collective conscience is more abstract, embodies repressive law, which imposes not severe penalities for rule infractions but seeks only a return to the condition that would have prevailed had the rule infractions not occurred, and stresses the dignity, rights, and individuality of all people.

Organic and mechanical solidarity are alike in that the proximate integrative force is the power embodied in the moral rules generated through interaction. However, the cause of interaction differs. In mechanical solidarity interaction results from mutual attraction, which in turn is proportional to similarity: the greater the similarity (likeness) the greater the mutual attraction, the higher the rate of interaction, the stronger the moral rules, and the greater the solidarity. Durkheim also notes reciprocal effects: the stronger the solidarity, the stronger the moral rules (collective conscience), the greater the similarities, and on as before. The basis of organic soidarity is complementary differences that denote complementary interests, that is, interests that each party seeks to promote through interaction. Durkheim argues that the greater the complementary interests, the greater the mutual attraction, the higher the rate of interaction, the stronger the moral rules, and the greater the solidarity. Organic and mechanical solidarity are different in that one is proportional to likenesses, the other to differences. They are the same in that the strength of each is proportional to the rate of interaction, interaction being the process through which moral rules are generated.

In contrast, Tocqueville traces solidarity to self-interest: Interest engenders the interaction that creates community (Figure 5, Chapter 2). The two theorists agree, however, that it is interaction that creates solidarity and that, consequently, the latter varies proportionately with the former.

Their common understanding of the relationship between interaction and solidarity must be understood in the context of differences separating them. In terms of Durkheim's understanding of the individual and the social as opposing forces, the greater power of emergent moral rules explains their ability to overcome and control opposing but less powerful individual forces. As social forces moral rules cause individuals to act in service of social (group) interest. Although social life benefits individuals, social interests also oppose the individual interests of group members. For Tocqueville individuals come to care about one another through contact. Durkheim locates solidarity in an emergent social power, Tocqueville in individuals' mutual concern.

In Durkheim's model of mechanical solidarity, similarities, likenesses, and commonalities, and in the organic model complementary interests, lead to interaction. The organic model converges with Tocqueville: interest → interaction → solidarity. Many commentators (for example, Parsons, 1968: 318; Nisbet, 1966: 86; 1974: 128) note that subsequent to *Division* the organic model dropped out of Durkheim's theory as he increasingly came to equate solidarity with the collective conscience and mechanical solidarity. Opponents of this view sometimes argue that Durkheim's increasingly exclusive use of the mechanical model reflects no theoretical change but only a shift in his empirical focus, for example, *The Elementary Forms* (1965) analyzes primitive society, which Durkheim (for example, 1960: 70-110) had always said was integrated mechanically. However, this argument overlooks the tension between (1) Durkheim's basic theoretical premises, which assert that, given their inherent opposition, the relative strength of social and individual forces varies inversely and (2) the underlying purpose of the model of organic solidarity, which was to explain how an individual factor (individual differences, individuality, and the expression of individual self-interest), could vary proportionately with solidarity (Durkheim, 1960: 37-38). This argument also slights the many difficulties Durkheim encounters in drawing a consistent, clear-cut distinction between organic and mechanical solidarity and the reasons underlying these difficulties. Nor does it explain the almost complete absence of the organic model in, for instance, *Suicide*, where not only in his general discussions of modern society but also in his analysis of bureaucratic institutions such as the military, Durkheim uses the mechanical rather than the organic model to explain varying levels of integration and regulation and, ultimately, varying social suicide rates. Insofar as Durkheim relied increasingly on a mechanical model of solidarity, this movement constitutes increasing divergence from Tocqueville on the source of the interaction that generates solidarity.

Both Tocqueville and Durkheim are concerned with the opposite of community and solidarity, labeled anomie by Durkheim. For Durkheim anomie is a condition of low regulation (integration, solidarity), weak moral rules, and inadequate social control. Under these conditions behavior is governed not by morality and social necessities but by egoistically defined self-interest. This breakdown of the social order produces the conditions Durkheim disliked: egoism, anomie, disorder, use of force, conflict, deviance, immorality, and injustice.

Both men attribute anomie to the same cause, insufficient interaction, and their historical accounts of its origin overlap. *Division* struggles to explain anomie in contemporary society. No doubt largely in the interest of showing how solidarity and individuality grow *pari passu* during the course of social evolution (Durkheim, 1960: 37-38), *Division* (37-38, 173) says that organic solidarity is stronger than mechanical solidarity. Nonetheless, it contains numerous indications that the reverse is true. *Division* contrasts the harsh, emotional sanctions demanded by the repressive law of primitive society with the mild, dispassionate sanctions specified by the restitutive law of modern society. Primitive society is portrayed as highly integrated, whereas modern society's lack of integration is Durkheim's greatest concern. *Division's* (1960: 1-31) famous proposal for the reconstitution of occupational groups advocates strengthening modern society with an infusion of solidarity that, partly mechanical and partly organic, is nonetheless predominately mechanical: "What we especially see in the occupational group is a moral power capable of containing the individual egos, of maintaining a spirited sentiment of common solidarity in the consciousness of all the workers." (Durkheim, 1960: 10). The only breakdowns of social order and morality *Division* (1960: 353-395) identifies are the anomic and the other abnormal forms of the division of labor in modern society. *Suicide* (1951: 152-216, 241-276) further documents the widespread egoism and anomie that undermine the contemporary moral order.

Division (1960: 353-373) cites three examples of the anomic division of labor: industrial or commercial crises and failures, the conflict between capital and labor, and the intellectual division of labor in science that prevents it from forming an integrated whole. *Suicide* (1951: 241-276) cites two kinds of anomie, each with its acute and chronic versions. Economic crises produce acute economic anomie. The diminution of religion's, civil authority's, and the occupational group's control over economic, especially industrial relations, produces chronic economic anomie. Widowhood causes acute domestic anomie, and the weakening of the social control embodied in marriage as an institution causes chronic domestic anomie.

Durkheim views most anomie as a consequence of the breakdown of social control in recent centuries. Tocqueville views it as a product of the transition from aristocratic to democratic society. Bound by aristocratic society's hierarchy to a station and its lifestyle, people accept their position and do not yearn for what tradition and society deny them. Destroying that hierarchy, democratic society frees people to want whatever society makes available.

Tocqueville and Durkheim state similar social psychologies of anomie. "Happiness consists in the correspondence of our wishes to our powers" (Tocquevile, 1872, 1: 139). Or, in Durkheim's (1951: 246) more famous formulation: "No living being can be happy . . . unless his needs are sufficiently proportioned to his means." Durkheim explains that people's social existence inculcates in them inherently expandable and therefore insatiable needs, goals, and desires. Only social control scales them down, thereby permitting their satisfaction and preventing the development of a disjunction between the means and needs. Tocqueville feels that with restraints removed democratic people see nothing but limitless horizons before them. Ever fearful that time will run out before they have had their fill, they hurry to earn and experience as much as possible. Durkheim's anomic person experiences disgust, irritation, anger, and disappointment; Tocqueville's restless anxiety.

Durkheim (1951: 323) analyzes anomie and closely related egoism as symptoms of the malaise of his day and identifies each as a cause of suicide. Tocqueville (1969: 538) considers suicide in France and madness in America as different symptoms of the tension-induced malaise caused by the disparity between the desires inculcated by equality and the means it provides for satisfying them. If both men were concerned about anomie, Durkheim's concern was greater. Anomie is the opposite of what Durkheim values, integration, order, and morality. For Tocqueville anomie is characteristic of democratic society and is linked to the individualism and materialism which threatens freedom. As a constant source of discontent, it exacts a toll on the individual. Nonetheless, it could, as in America, be combined with political freedom and, as a source of irrepressible energy, promote national prosperity and greatness.

Freedom. If to assess their views on solidarity is to nudge Tocqueville in the direction of Durkheim's central concern, to assess their perspectives on freedom is to nudge Durkheim toward Tocqueville's central concern. Although both men were liberals committed to freedom, Durkheim struggled to show how his theory of integration also demonstrated that in the modern world integration and freedom grew proportionately.

Durkheim holds that, divorced from society, people are controlled by biological forces. Only by opposing these forces with social forces can they free themselves. Nonetheless, the social individual is not necessarily free. In primitive society the "liberating" social forces are so strong as to themselves negate individuality and freedom. Modern society poses multiple problems. Power may be so unevenly distributed that some groups seriously curtail the freedom of other groups. Social regulation and integration themselves may be so weak as to leave people prey, not to biological forces, but to the expanding needs or meaninglessness that in extreme cases causes suicide (Durkheim, 1951: 152-216, 241-276). The image of freedom as a product of counterbalancing individual and social forces is incomplete as a theory of freedom.

Another Durkheimian theme is that under certain conditions people will come to recognize the benefit and necessity of subordinating themselves to society, which is good and from which they get the best part of themselves. Such understanding leads people to submit themselves voluntarily to societal control. This solution to the problem of freedom and control is quintessential Durkheim in that, far from postulating any tension between the two, it locates freedom in subordination to social forces. It is also reminiscent of that element in Tocqueville's theory linking freedom with subordination to authority. Ultimately, Durkheim's approach rests on his assumptions that science can determine both what modern society and our values should be. Having done all this and representing the highest form of human rationality, science will acquire the authority enabling it to persuade people to submit voluntarily to the necessary social control of a just, rational society. However, Durkheim offers no convincing evidence that the possibilities he envisions are either occurring or are likely to occur. As a theory of modern society Durkheim's account is no more convincing than Marx's location of freedom in future utopian society.

Durkheim argues that the relationship between freedom and integration in primitive society is the obverse of that in modern society. The primitives' *social* life negates individuality and freedom. However, unlike modern social science, Durkheim defines most of their lives as nonsocial, including, for instance, everyday life among the Arunta (Australian aborigines). In their nonsocial lives primitives are free of social control, yet remain subject to control by the nonsocial forces inherent in human existence.

If Durkheim denies that primitives are free, his first book (Durkheim, 1960) seeks to show that individuality or freedom and solidarity grew *pari passu* during social evolution and are proportionately related in modern society. The Preface to *Division* reflects Durkheim's awareness that the reconciliation of freedom and solidarity poses a difficult analytic problem: How can the individual "be at once more individual and more solidary? Certainly, these two movements, *contradictory as they appear,* develop in parallel fashion. . . . What resolves this apparent antimony" is the transformation from mechanical to organic solidarity (Durkheim, 1960: 37-38; emphasis added).

Durkheim's theory of organic solidarity asserts that the greater the individuality (individual differences), the greater are complementary differences, mutual dependence, the potential benefits derived from and the need for exchange, mutual attraction, the rate of interaction, and the stronger the moral rules. In short, individuality and solidarity vary proportionately.

This solution to the "apparent antimony" between individuality, individual pursuit of self-interest, and freedom, on the one hand, and solidarity, on the other, may appear satisfactory. Certainly it continues to satisfy many commentators. Nonetheless, it remains problematic. Consistent with his view of the individual and the social as opposing forces, when Durkheim wishes to emphasize the strength of organic solidarity he cites the moral rules that constitute its proximate *source;* when he seeks to show that individuality and freedom are proportionately related to organic solidarity, he appeals to individual differences as its *basis.* However, if differences are the basis of organic solidarity, ultimately they lead to the generation of the moral rules that as social forces control the individual. What Durkheim fails to demonstrate is that freedom and control increase simultaneously.[4]

Both theorists (Tocqueville more than Durkheim) are famous for their emphasis on the importance of secondary groups. Both in *Division's* "Preface to the Second Edition: Some Notes on Occupational

---

4. Both in *Division* and elsewhere (for example, Durkheim, 1973a) Durkheim appeals to changes in the content of the collective conscience to explain why mechanical solidarity is inversely and organic solidarity proportionately related to individuality and freedom. However, this thesis creates numerous problems: (1) Appeal to the collective conscience as an increasingly important basis of solidarity in modern society contradicts Durkheim's assertions that it grows weaker in modern society and that organic solidarity, based on something other than the collective conscience, increasingly replaces mechanical solidarity (Durkheim, 1960: 37-38, 167, 170-174, 283, 361, 364). Identification of the collective conscience as a source of organic solidarity (2) is inconsistent with many of the contrasts Durkheim draws between mechanical and organic solidarity, and (3) in blurring the distinction between them, undermines many of his attempts to show how and why one is proportionately and the other inversely related to individuality. (4) Ultimately this appeal does not answer Durkheim's question because, as before, it fails to show how social forces and individuality can vary proportionately.

Groups" and elsewhere, Durkheim (1902/1960: 1-46; 1958; 1951: 378-384) advocates the establishment of such groups, specifically the reconstitution of strong occupational groups to overcome the anomie and egoism of modern society.

> A society composed of an infinite number of unorganized individuals, that a hypertrophied State is forced to oppress and contain, constitutes a veritable sociological monstrosity. For collective activity is always too complex to be able to be expressed through the single and unique organ of the State. . . . Where the State is the only environment in which men can live communal lives, they inevitably lose contact, become detached, and thus society disintegrates. A nation can be maintained only if, between the State and the individual, there is intercalated a whole series of secondary groups near enough to the individuals to attract them strongly in their sphere of action and drag them . . . into the general torrent of social life [Durkheim, 1960: 28].

Social scientists more familiar with Durkheim than Tocqueville may not realize the degree to which this passage expresses ideas worked out carefully by the latter.

Professional Ethics and Civic Morals (1958), Durkheim's major work on the state, locates freedom in balanced forces, which free individuals versus unbalanced forces, which tyrannize them. Freed of external restraint societies are inherently despotic (Durkheim, 1958: 61). In earlier times everything pertaining to the individual, personality, interests, private concerns, and personal views, beliefs, and aspirations, were deemed insignificant. Rather, absorbed into the mass of society individuals succumbed meekly to social pressures and willingly subordinated their personal interests to those of the group (Durkheim, 1958: 56). The main function of the state, then, is to free individuals from the otherwise tyrannical control of its constituent groups. As the state grows stronger, individuality develops as individuals become freer and more respected (Durkheim, 1958: 57, 62). Far from state intervention being inherently despotic it alleviates existing tyrannies. But might not, Durkheim (1958: 63) asks, the state in turn become a repressive leveler? Yes, and such tyranny is even worse than that imposed by local groups, because, removed from local wishes, the state violates them. Thus just as only an opposing force can avert the potential tyranny of secondary groups, the same is true of the state. Each opposes and balances the power of the other: "It is out of this conflict of social forces that individual liberties are born" (Durkheim, 1958: 63).

We find, then, many common themes in Tocqueville and Durkheim: (1) viable secondary groups that meet the needs of their members promote an active social life, prosperity, community, and morality; (2) the state is too removed from individuals and the differences among them, and from local variations and contingencies to take them into account; consequently, when the state controls local affairs it does so in a clumsy, arbitrary way that undermines what secondary groups promote; (3) a legitimate state is a source of liberty; (4) balanced power is the structural source of freedom; and (5) the only way to balance the power of the state is to oppose it with a competing power; the best way to do this is with strong secondary groups.

Though the two Frenchmen partly converge, their analyses also differ. Durkheim assesses the degree to which the individual is tyrannized by any social power. Equally concerned with political and nonpolitical threats to freedom, he postulates the tyrannical potential of both local (secondary) groups and the state. Tocqueville also recognizes the potential tyranny of such groups. For instance, in democratic society the local tyranny of the majority curtails freedom. However, Tocqueville feels local social control, whether of peer over peer in democratic society, or peer over peer and superior over inferior in aristocratic society, is inevitable. In addition, he believes that the more local the institution or group the more individuals molded them to their own interests. Accordingly, Tocqueville explains variation in freedom as a function of the strength of local groups relative to that of the national government and its potentially centralized administration. For Durkheim freedom exists where two forces impinging on people conflict and partially negate each other and for Tocqueville where viable secondary groups balance the power of the state to create political freedom.[5]

There are enough common themes in their treatments of freedom to hypothesize Tocqueville's influence on Durkheim. Although Durkheim (for example, 1960: 43-44) only occasionally mentions Tocqueville, more frequently he fails to cite him even where a reference might be expected—neither the "Preface to the Second Edition" of *Division* (1960: 1-31) nor *Professional Ethics* (1958) mentions Tocqueville. Neither does he identify Tocqueville as an influence on his thinking about freedom, the state, and secondary groups. However plausible, unless further evidence is forthcoming, the assertion of Tocqueville's influence on Durkheim's thinking about these matters must remain hypothetical.

5. The difference between the perspectives on freedom developed in *Professional Ethics* (Durkheim, 1958) and the theory of organic solidarity is striking. *Professional Ethics* locates freedom in opposing social forces that neutralize each other; the theory of organic solidarity not only postulates no conflict between social control and individual freedom but asserts that solidarity and freedom vary proportionately. This change is simply one additional indication that subsequent to *Division* Durkheim dropped his model of organic solidarity.

Religion. Their views on religion, which interested them for much the same reason, are both similar and different. On the grounds that it has real causes and consequences and corresponds to real needs, all of which are social, Durkheim (1965) concludes that religion is a social reality. Further rejecting the contention that religion is false, Durkheim argues that religious beliefs represent realities and religion itself meets enduring human needs. Primitives were not deceived in their belief in the existence of powerful forces controlling them. They were mistaken only in locating the source of that power in a symbol and in failing to understand that the power actually lay in what the symbol represented, namely, society. Stressing their underlying continuity, Durkheim says that religion and science address the same basic realities. Rather than science as truth replacing religion as falsehood, as a more adequate representation of reality, science increasingly supplants religion commensurate with increased human understanding of the world.

Tocqueville feels no need to demonstrate that religion is a social reality in order to legitimate a sociological explanation of it nor does he argue that religious beliefs are generally true. Rather, he believes that many religions are false. He accepts Christianity's basic moral teachings as true and as a standard by which to judge other religions. Asserting these truths, he does not attempt to demonstrate them scientifically.

In the face of pervasive secularization Durkheim struggled to locate in modern society the strong religion he (1965) considered a *sine qua non* of a viable society. The weakening of Catholic, Protestant, and Jewish religious communities (Durkheim, 1951: 152-170) was just one more aspect of the anomie and egoism that constituted the malaise of the modern age. Durkheim (1960: 172, 400, 407; 1973a) argues that with the evolutionary growth of individuality the individual becomes the object of a cult whose beliefs stress the value and dignity of the individual. However, although he (1973a) increasingly came to view this cult or religion of humanity as the decisive component of modern society's collective conscience, he also bemoans contemporary society's lack of religious integration. *The Elementary Forms* (Durkheim, 1965: 475) asserts that society will once again experience the "creative effervescence" from which arise new beliefs to guide humanity. He saw the French Revolution as an example that, however, proved only temporary (1965: 476). Characteristically applying classic functionalist logic, an optimistic Durkheim predicts a rebirth of religion. However, he does not underestimate the seriousness of the problem—"the old gods are growing old or already dead, and others are not yet born"—and he acknowledges that "because we are going through a stage of transition and moral mediocrity" it is difficult to imagine what the regenerative religious "feasts and ceremonies of the future could consist in" (Durkheim, 1965: 475).

Durkheim's evolutionary approach virtually equates primitive society and religion. In the beginning there was religion from which other institutions were born through differentiation; subtracting it, little remains. Durkheim's image of society as a structural-functional system invites analysis of the relationships between religion and the other parts of society and society itself. However, it is hard to apply this kind of analysis to primitive society which, as a structural-functional system, is an oddity—a system with but one part.

Durkheim's conception of society as above all collective representations suggests less the reciprocal influence of religion and society than that religion is the vital core of society. Because their efficacy, including control over individuals, is proportional to their strength, the key variable aspect of collective representations is strength. Strong collective representations are religious representations. Religious solidarity is the primordial mechanical solidarity. Whether we seek the decisive component of the collective conscience of modern society, the ultimate source of mechanical solidarity, the original social institution, the core of society defined as collective representations, or the strongest social forces we are led to the same institution—religion. Appropriately, Durkheim's last major work (1912/1965), his magnum opus, was on this subject.

Durkheim's functional approach to religion focuses on its positive contributions. Religion meets both society's and humans' enduring social needs. Cognitively, religion is a cosmology; it provides the common symbols, beliefs, and understandings without which social life is impossible. The source of society's strongest moral rules, religion is the primordial basis of social integration.

Tocqueville often assesses religion in human or pragmatic, functionalist terms. He emphasizes Christianity's positive contributions from its birth to the modern period. Providing people with a cosmology and grounding for their values, Christianity also promotes community by stressing mutual obligations and spiritual values. In the modern world Christianity was a necessary antidote to democracy's materialism.

If Tocqueville often emphasizes the positive effects of religion, particularly Christianity, he also notes religion's dysfunctions, especially those of non-Christian, Eastern religions. He considers Mohammedanism to be "the primary cause of the now visible decadence of the Islamic world" (Tocqueville, 1968b: 212). He is even harder on Hinduism, which was guilty of a cardinal vice, undermining public virtue. By splitting India into castes Hinduism made her prey to the worst fate that can befall a nation, foreign conquest, of which the British rule there provides only the most recent historical example. In general, Hinduism is largely reponsible for India's backwardness and decadence. Durkheim focuses on the way in which any society or group molded, controlled, and benefited its individual members. His functionalism emphasizes the positive contributions of parts to the whole. Durkheim shows how religion controls and shapes individuals and integrates society, but fails to analyze it as a resource enabling some to dominate others. In contrast, Tocqueville attends to the way power and interest structures influence groups and institutions. In Western Europe the church had to reach an accommodation with the state and, as in France's old regime, sometimes allowed its pursuit of power and exercise of political authority to compromise its spiritual mission. Their resentment of the way the church exercised its political power caused the French to become first politically alienated from it and then generally alienated from it and religion as well. If *The Old Regime* does not claim that the church was on balance dysfunctional, Tocqueville makes clear that it fell far short of realizing its potential for good.

As an integral part of society, to remain viable in America religion had to accommodate to democratic values. Denying the church political authority, the separation of church and state benefited religion by enabling it to minimize its direct political entanglements. Tocqueville feels that in America religion has found the best way to remain true to its mission.

If both Tocqueville and Durkheim claim that, in Tocqueville's (1969: 515; see also p. 645) words, "feelings and ideas are renewed, the heart enlarged, and the understanding developed only by the reciprocal action of men one upon another," Durkheim provides the fuller account of how interaction generates solidarity. His earlier works often simply assert the relationship between interaction and solidarity or intimate the theory that *The Elementary Forms* details. That statement clarifies Durkheim's characteristic emphasis on interaction and the importance of commonalities. His theory of religion also provides many of his fullest accounts of moral rules, social control, and collective representations. Religious rituals give birth to and strengthen morality and religious beliefs, create and recreate society, and infuse it with the power that makes it a force and without which it withers and dies.

Durkheim's theory of religion explains all these things. Religion is a system of mutually dependent and mutually reinforcing rites, beliefs, and symbols that generate, embody, and symbolize social force. Religious beliefs explain and justify the rites. Their ability to mandate them is proportional to their strength. Rites generate religious beliefs. Beliefs, ideas, sentiments, and representations are forces (Durkheim,

1965n: 260). What happens to these forces when they meet as individuals interact depends on their relative similarity. In conflicting and enfeebling each other, dissimilar individual sentiments and beliefs fail to form and revitalize collective representations, which consequently languish. However, similar individual sentiments fuse to form collective representations that are powerful because they embody the power of each of the individual representations the fusion of which creates them. Repetitive, stereotyped ritual movements symbolize beliefs. The very similarity of these movements increases the similarity of the individual ideas they symbolize, and, by moving those ideas to the forefront of consciousness, makes ritual participants aware that they hold the same ideas. Under these conditions individual representations fuse to form collective representations. Sacred material objects, for example, totems or flags, symbolize the group or society and remind individuals of their commonalities and collective existence. As symbols these objects perpetuate collective sentiments even when the group is dispersed and when individual, profane activities and beliefs weaken collective beliefs. When individuals first come together after a period of dispersion collective representations are weak, and individual representations strong. Material symbols help initiate ritual behavior by reminding individuals of their common beliefs and ritual obligations. The resulting rituals strengthen symbols by generating and strengthening the collective representations and social forces they represent.

Both Durkheim and Tocqueville treat religion as a cosmology, as a source of the shared beliefs and understandings without which society is impossible, and as a source of morality and moral integration. Though Durkheim was a functionalist, in many ways Tocqueville's functionalist approach to religion was more viable. Tocqueville's does not reify collective concepts such as collective representations and society, never uses a reified conception of a powerful, self-conscious society to explain the link between functional necessity and institutional existence, is as sensitive to religion's negative as to its positive functions, and analyzes religion in the context of the societal struggle for power. If Durkheim's conception of society as a system views religion as one part of a system, in practice Tocqueville's analyses are often more consistent with this view than are Durkheim's. Whereas Tocqueville treats religion as one of many institutions that reciprocally influence each other, Durkheim's view of religion in primitive society as *the* institution leaves little room for analyzing reciprocal relations. In analyzing contemporary society Tocqueville often does more to trace religion's reciprocal relations with other institutions than does Durkheim who, stressing the functional necessity of religion, is more likely to bemoan the lack of an adequate religion and to stress the benefits to be expected from its resurgence.

Writing more extensively about religion than does Tocqueville, Durkheim's most valuable contribution, one that goes beyond Tocqueville, is his analysis of the way in which it integrates groups and society. Durkheim's theory of religion and ritual solidarity has influenced not only functionalists, including Parsons (1968), Radcliffe-Brown (1952), Bellah (1970), and Warner (1959), but even less likely candidates such as Collins (1975: 153-154), who incorporates Durkheim's theory of ritual solidarity into his contemporary statement of *Conflict Sociology*.[6]

Morality. Durkheim asserts the social character of morality. Like all living organisms society has needs. Specifying the conditions of social health, moral rules prescribe how humans must act if societal needs are to be met. Morality originates in society and serves social interests; society is both its source and object. Agreeing that it originates in social life, Tocqueville (1969: 616) defines morality (or honor) as the standards used to judge right and wrong. The functionalist strain in Tocqueville is reminiscent of Durkheim: "There are some universal and permanent needs of mankind on which moral laws are based" (Tocqueville, 1969: 616). Again, like Durkheim, he (1969: 618) feels that the varying needs of different societies give rise to varying concepts of morality to meet those needs. Although both men recognize that different classes or groups in society may have different values, their approach to these differences vary. Seeking the bases of societal integration, Durkheim emphasizes the morality common to an entire society and the ways in which the functionally compatible moralities of different groups help integrate those groups into the larger whole. Tocqueville notes that different classes or groups in society typically not only share a common morality but also subscribe to different, group-specific moralities that can cause conflict among them. For Durkheim morality is the essential source of social integration; for Tocqueville, though an essential source of integration, morality may also be a source of conflict.

Durkheim is more accepting and Tocqueville more critical of societal moralities. Durkheim defines society as good. Humans get the best part of themselves through society and, indeed, are raised above their biological nature and the level of animals only by social life. As parts of the whole (society), people prosper when society prospers and suffers when it suffers. Viewing societal moralities as responsive to the needs of the societies in which they are found, Durkheim accepts these varying moralities. Indeed, he proposes a sociological science of ethics that would show the rational necessity of accepting the appropriateness of

6. For a discussion of Durkheim's influence on Guy Swanson, Mary Douglas, and Claude Levi-Strauss, see Ian Hamnett (1984).

these moralities and of the morality appropriate for modern society just as we are rationally bound to accept the other findings of science.

Tocqueville's approach is less sociologistic and less relativistic. He does not view the moralities of different societies as invariably functionally appropriate for that society and therefore good. Neither does he define morality in terms of what is good for society. Individuals have moral claims on the group, as well as a range of claims beyond those concerning the relationship between the individual and the group, and all societies must be evaluated in terms of the degree to which they promote the paramount values of justice and individual freedom. Nor does Tocqueville propose a science of ethics to determine morality. Social science addresses the social origins and consequences, only some of which are functional, of values. However, the moral worth of varying moralities is not a function of their objective, scientifically determined furtherance of societal interests. Rather, the moral assessment of values is achieved by evaluating them in terms of the moral standards and truths contained in moral-philosophical systems of religious or other nonscientific origin. Using his own values to assess the moralities of different societies, Tocqueville found much that repelled him.

"Every society is despotic," writes Durkheim (1958: 61). This despotism is both natural and necessary if societies are to exist. Individuals do not experience it as oppressive any more than they feel weighed down by the earth's atmosphere. Having been raised in society the individual wants what it wants and accepts "without difficulty the state of subjection to which he finds himself reduced." In contrast, Tocqueville (1969: 252, 436, 693) rejects as tyrannical any source of absolute power.

Both authors are concerned about understanding morality in order to promote the morality each endorses. As liberals, they use the same basic values, particularly freedom and justice, to evaluate modern society. Viewing it as permeated by egoism, anomie, and materialism, each is alarmed by modern society's lack of morality. Although each treats these concerns partly in terms of ideal types of modern society, they differ on the relationship between these ideal types and reality. Tocqueville's ideal type analysis of democratic society links equality and tyranny; Durkheim (1960) argues that organic society is normally just, integrated, and free. The societies they examine sometimes depart in opposite ways from these ideal types. Durkheim's empirical instances of modern, industrial, organic society are unintegrated and deficient in freedom and justice. Tocqueville's America is not tyrannical but (politically) free. Finally, emphasizing what modern societies have in common, Durkheim sees less variation among them. Tocqueville contrasts America and France in terms of morality, freedom, justice, and the other variables of greatest concern to him.

The two authors' analyses of the morality of premodern and modern societies differ. Perpetuated by religion and collective reactions to violations of repressive law, Durkheim sees in primitive society a strong collective conscience embodying strong morality. Given a powerful society and the virtual absence of individuality, there is no conflict between the demands of individuality and social integration. Morality in modern society causes Durkheim his greatest problems. Structurally homogenous, primitive society is tailor made for Durkheim's theoretical perspectives, but what of the disparate groups and functions in modern society, with their different and possibly conflicting interests and values? Durkheim's theory of organic solidarity seeks to explain how such groups will be morally integrated. However, which of his accounts of modern society is more convincing: this analysis or his empirical description, which acknowledges conflict, domination, exploitation, meaningless work, economic crises, egoism, anomie, the lack of freedom, injustice, and other manifestations of the "abnormal" forms of the division of labor?

For Durkheim, strong moral rules—those that inspire awe, command authority, and produce universal, unquestioning obedience—are religious. What explains the existence of the sacred—and hence, ultimately, religion—is the generation of powerful but unexplained social forces. Religion originates in the strong moral forces created by religious ritual.

If religion explains the strong moral rules in primitive society, when might people in modern society gather in the presence of common material symbols, sustain high rates of interaction consisting of the stereotyped symbolic movements representing common beliefs, and otherwise meet the conditions of religious ritual? Durkheim struggles unsuccessfully to answer this question, and is far clearer about the consequences of the absence in modern society of the functional equivalent of the religious ritual of the primitives than about the specifics of such an equivalent. He hopes for some kind of religious rebirth but acknowledges his own uncertainty about when, where, and how that might take place. Hence, the theoretical tension in Durkheim's work. He asserts the strength of organic solidarity, yet his theory of religion suggests that, shorn of religious origin and grounding, moral rules in modern society will lack the strength religion imparts to primitive morality.

In lieu of his emphasis on religion in primitive society, Durkheim's analyses of modern society considers institutions potentially capable of strengthening its moral rules. He writes extensively about *Moral Education* (1961; see also Durkheim, 1965), *Professional Ethics and Civic Morals* (1958), and occupational groups. In each case there are problems. For instance, education is an important agent of socialization controlled by the state, but as a part of the whole, education reflects society itself. If that society is deficient in morality, can education be expected to compensate fully? Again, consistent with his organic image of society Durkheim proposes constituting groups consistent with its functional divisions, but occupational groups are weak or nonexistent. At best they have potential. Durkheim has trouble explaining the discrepancy between what his theory predicts, strong morality in a healthy society, and what he actually observes, weak morality in unhealthy societies. Attributing all the undesirable discrepancies to abnormal conditions, he is unable to argue convincingly that what he views as normal coincides with the empirically expected.

If morality in modern society causes Durkheim his greatest problems, premodern Europe fails to maximize certain values important to Tocqueville. Where community exists it curbs excesses of power. Even so, in premodern Europe power is too unevenly distributed to make society just. Domination is the price the lower orders have to pay for protection and community. Modern society is more just and America shows that political freedom can coexist with equality.

Despite contrary views about the level of freedom in primitive society, both Tocqueville and Durkheim approve of primitive morality. Though Durkheim feels that primitives are not free, he approves of primitive morality as strong and functional. Tocqueville commends primitive society for its freedom and describes Amerindians as free, proud, and dignified.

Tocqueville and Durkheim are liberals who value justice and seek to combine social control and freedom. Each felt that morality must reflect the necessities of social life and each is concerned about egoism and other threats to the modern moral order; but they approach morality from different starting points. Durkheim feels that morality serves collective interests, whether that of a two-person group or that of the modern nation-state. In contrast, the distinction between nonpolitical and political morality is basic to Tocqueville, who is concerned that the individual's concern for a small group of close relatives and friends expand to include a political concern for the public good. Defining society as an emergent phenomenon, Durkheim focuses on the relative strength of opposed individual and social forces. He begins with society, its reality, requirements, and morality, and tries to show how in modern society social necessities can be reconciled with individual freedom. Developing different analyses of the relationship between social control and freedom, Durkheim most frequently locates order, justice, and freedom in society's ability to contain the expression of individual self-interest. Rather than assert the necessity to suppress self-interest,

Tocqueville specifies the conditions and structures, which by enlightening and expanding it make its pursuit compatible with the other values he seeks to promote. Beginning not with society but with his paramount value, freedom, Tocqueville seeks to demonstrate not merely that freedom is compatible with his other values but, indeed, that the conditions that maximize freedom also maximize order, community, authority, prosperity, and justice.

TOCQUEVILLE AND THE OTHER THEORISTS

Durkheim

If comparing Tocqueville and Durkheim produces a mixture of similarities and dissimilarities, and if Tocqueville and Durkheim share similar concerns, often analyze the same phenomena, and sometimes develop analyses of them that are more similar than might be anticipated given underlying differences in their perspectives, they remain separated by fundamental differences. Durkheim is an evolutionary structural-functionalist and a social realist. Viewing all the world as systems of forces, he treats the individual and society as opposing forces. Taking society as good, he analyzes phenomena in terms of the extent to which they further or undermine what he takes to be societal interests—above all, social integration. Reifying society and other collective concepts such as collective representations, he describes how the intervention of society as a rational, self-conscious power explains the link between the functional necessity of social institutions and their existence. Durkheim overemphasizes positive as opposed to negative functions, which were explained away as the consequence of abnormal conditions. Tocqueville does not share these perspectives.

Durkheim views collective representations as the vital core of society and moral consensus as the source of social integration. Tocqueville (1969: 373) also views ideas as the core and consensus as a sine qua non of society. His assertion of such ideas has led some commentators to classify him along with Durkheim as a consensus theorist. Indeed, he has been identified as the historical progenitor of contemporary consensus theory with its repudiation of perspectives that emphasize the importance of power and coercion (Horowitz, 1967: 269). This one-sided view derives from a selective attention to his works. In particular, *Democracy* constitutes its foundation, while *The Old Regime, Recollections*, and his other writings are ignored. Just as *Democracy* finds consensus and community in America, *The Old Regime* explains how increasingly prevalent egoism, conflict, and force culminated in the French Revolution; and *Recollections* describes the legacy of France's divisive, revolutionary heritage. Theorists like Bendix (1977, 1978) and Collins (1968, 1975), familiar with his work generally, do not treat him as a consensus theorist. Comparing nations, Tocqueville seeks the causes and consequences of varying levels of community and consensus. To acknowledge this concern is not to deny his concern with power, authority, and coercion. To the contrary, in Tocqueville these concerns are fused; he explains community and power in terms of each other. Specifically, Tocqueville links authority to community and force to egoism.

Marx

Along with other conflict theorists, both Tocqueville and Marx see society as a hierarchically structured system of power in which individuals and groups seek to use available resources in a competitive struggle to realize their interests. Concerned with the sources of power and the way in which people use it to dominate and coerce one another, each is also concerned with the bases and effects of community and restraints on the exercise of coercive power. Beyond these similarities lies an equally important difference in their respective images of society. Whereas Marx employs a unidimensional approach to social stratification that asserts the primacy of the economic order, Tocqueville, like Weber[7] (1968: 926-940), employs a multidimensional approach that distinguishes among the social (status), the economic (class), and the political power orders of society. Each sphere influences and is influenced by the others but none can be reduced to another.

Tocqueville does not share certain distinctively Marxian perspectives on change and revolution. Marx asserts the dialectical nature of social

7. If Weber were added to this comparison, in terms of the perspectives employed throughout this book Tocqueville is often least like Durkheim and most like Weber. In terms of contrasts developed in this chapter, and specifically in this summary comparison of Marx and Tocqueville, what is treated here as a Marx-Tocqueville contrast equally contrasts both Tocqueville and Weber with Marx.

I briefly note some important similarities between Tocqueville and Weber: the distinction between material and ideal interests; multidimensional (class, states, and political power) and a state and society image of society; the flexible, multicausal approach to history; action theory; rejection of views of social structures as something more than the sum of the behavior of the individual actors who constitute them; the rejection of the reification of collective concepts; the concern to generalize and use abstract concepts, generalizations, and other analytic resources in a way that does not negate the individuality of given historical actors, events, and configurations; the concern with freedom, especially in the modern Western world; the centralization and decentralization of administration (Tocqueville) or bureaucratization (Weber).

reality: Reality consists of systems of forces; forces engender opposing forces (their own negation), change occurs as a result of conflict between these opposing forces. These metatheoretical perspectives assert the continuous operation of the dialectic and hence the inevitability of conflict and change (Marx, 1977: 202). Marx (1978: 302) is concerned not only with existence and being but also with development and change. Adequate Marxian analysis of a given social formation requires tracing its historical development; analyzing its functioning; identifying the source of the internal contradictions and conflicts that will inevitably change it; and, based on this identification of the causes of change, assessing its likely direction.

For Marx the impetus for change originates in new, more productive ways of materially producing. In terms of his base-superstructure model, these new powers or forces of production conflict with and eventually transform the previously existing relations of production. Subsequently, the superstructure is also transformed. In terms of his class model of society, a new class representing these new powers of production comes into conflict with the ruling class representing the existing relations of production. The struggle for supremacy between these two classes is eventually won by the new class that, as the new ruling class, ultimately transforms the entire society in its image.

At its core, Marx's theory is a theory of society and history, that is, of social change. Marx asserts the revolutionary, as opposed to the peaceful or evolutionary nature of change. Class conflict builds until the forces of change overpower opposing forces and transform one type of society into another. In Western European history these types are (in chronological order): tribal, ancient, feudal, capitalist, and (future) communist society. Marx often seeks to explain how one type engendered its successor, for example, how feudalism gave birth to capitalism and, most particularly, how capitalism will inevitably be transformed into communism. His classification of societies into distinct evolutionary stages assumes the systemic nature of society. Specifically, the economic structure of society is the foundation of a distinctive type of society.

Marx's (1978: 143-145) critique of materialism and idealism reflects his distinctive epistemology. The materialists correctly emphasized the influence of people's material existence on their thought. The problem with materialism, however, is that in treating people as a product and as a passive object it does not understand society as their product and show how, through their own striving, people alter their circumstances. Though stressing the importance of ideas, idealism neglects the influence of material conditions on ideas and, in failing to break out of the realm of ideas, fails to engender the practical action changing society. In short, idealist and materialist "philosophers have only *interpreted* the world, in various ways; the point, however, is to *change* it."

Theory that is not put into practice remains as sterile as practice uninformed by theory. Marx proposes praxis or the union of theory and practice as the way to salvage the valid insights of materialism and idealism and overcome their shortcomings. "Man must prove the truth, that is, the reality and power . . . of his thinking in practice." This union of theory and practice is dialectical. By influencing behavior theoretical developments lead to new circumstances, which in turn lead to further theoretical development.

In capitalist society praxis means the union of Marxian theory with revolutionary proletarian activity. Existing material conditions cannot be transformed without a powerful material force. Guided both by the understanding resulting from the conditions of their existence and by Marxian theory, the proletariat becomes such a force. In helping the masses understand what must be done so that structural conditions will engender instead of impede the realization of human needs, communism becomes more than simply a set of possibly correct ideas; it becomes a force for change in the world. The truth of communism is tested by its efficacy. Insofar as these ideas lead to the understanding and revolutionary activity transforming capitalism into communist, utopian society and hence the conditions for the self-realization and freedom of all men, their power and reality is demonstrated; insofar as they do not this failure provides the basis for critique and revision. In activating and guiding practice, theory becomes an agent for change; in putting ideas into effect and thereby demonstrating their effects, practice becomes the test of theory.

Tocqueville does not subscribe to dialectical conception of social reality or the Marxian theory of history. Although he recognizes conflict as an important source of change, he does not identify it as the primary agent of change. Nor does Tocqueville argue that history culminates in future utopian society, that science can determine values, or that practice is the test of social scientific truth.

Extending well beyond the issue of the economic factor's primacy as a cause of social change, Tocqueville's disagreement with Marx's assertion of the primacy of the economic factor emerges repeatedly. Marx's unidimensional approach to social stratification is based on the assumption that economic power in the form of ownership and control of the means of production is the decisive form of social power. Asserting the primacy of society, specifically its economic structure, Marx analyzes the state as its outgrowth. For instance, "the executive of the modern State is but a committee for managing the common affairs of the whole bourgeoisie" (Marx, 1978: 475). (Of course, Marx, 1978: 594-617 also argues that the state and its bureaucracy, far from simply reflecting the social structure, under certain conditions becomes a partially independent force in its own right, capable of dominating society.) In summarizing his base-superstructure model Marx (1978: 4-5) begins with a discussion of the powers of production and ends with an examination of ideas and consciousness. "It is not the consciousness of men that determines their being but, on the contrary, their social being that determines their consciousness." In class terms "the ideas of the ruling class are in every epoch the ruling ideas" (Marx, 1978: 172-173). The class that owns and controls the means of production uses its derivative control of the "means of mental production" to establish an intellectual-ideological hegemony justifying society's basic social, economic, and political structures, including, of course, its own rule. Tocqueville agrees with Marx about the importance of ideas. Given their influence on behavior, ideas are weapons that all groups seek to use in the competitive struggle for advantage. Like all other power resources, ideas are one focal point of conflict. Yet, consistent with his multidimensional approach to social stratification, Tocqueville does not try to show why an economically dominant class will also be culturally and ideologically dominant. There may be no ideologically dominant class; rather, different classes and groups may exercise varying levels of ideological dominance in different (for example, economic, political, social, cultural) spheres. Again, insofar as one class achieves relative ideological dominance, that class need not also be economically dominant. In addition, instead of seeing ideas as ultimately an outgrowth of the underlying social structure, Tocqueville, asserting that ideas have a life of their own, feels that ideas and social structure reciprocally influence even while remaining partially autonomous of each other. Ideas cannot be understood merely as reflections of underlying interests, economic or otherwise. Ideas and ideal interests are just as real and important as material interests.

In sum, Marx and Tocqueville share an image of society as a hierarchically structured system of power in which individuals and groups vie for survival and supremacy. Especially in his more dogmatic, polemical works, Marx sometimes asserts the causal primacy of the economic factor. He often uses this hypothesis to organize his analyses. Tracing the influence of the economic structure of society, he seeks to assess the extent to which the hypothesis of its causal primacy is historically supported versus the extent to which it needs to be modified and supplemented, and if so, how and why. In contrast, Tocqueville postulates a multicausal world. Rather than assert the causal primacy of any single factor, he hypothesizes the importance of various factors the mutual relations of which combine partial mutual autonomy and reciprocal influence.

CONCLUSION

Perhaps because he claims no large following of devotees to overstate the case for him, Tocqueville's ideas exist in a live-and-let-live world. There are few attacks on him or in his name on others. He has been widely slighted but also greatly appreciated. Critiques of Tocqueville are generally moderate in tone. He has not been the subject of the kind of debates that, inherent to scholarship and initially instructive, becomes polemical and continues long past the point of diminishing returns. This contrasts sharply with other schools of thought in social science.

Perhaps the only unfortunate consequence of the relative lack of debate over Tocqueville is the absence of a comprehensive, appreciative but critical assessment of his work, particularly of his theory. No doubt, the widespread perception that he fails to employ, much less clearly state, a theory has militated against such a critique. The valid criticisms of his work are scarcely devastating. Often directed at the accuracy of his empirical assessments or otherwise only tangentially related to his theory of freedom, these criticisms have failed to identify serious theoretical shortcomings. Furthermore, comparison of Tocqueville to Marx and Durkheim suggests that he can stand comparison even with such exemplary theorists.

To the degree that I have successfully identified his theory, it now becomes a clearer target. Perhaps inclusion of more criticism of Tocqueville would help to achieve the appearance of having stated a balanced assessment. However, I have identified the criticisms that my analysis of his work suggests. If I offer no major criticisms of his theory, others may find reason to do so. Serious identification and assessment of major shortcomings in Tocqueville's theory have yet to begin.

4

Conclusion

Whatever their merits, theories that do not treat important phenomena fail. For many people, including those in the Western European tradition, freedom is a basic value. Indeed, Collins (1975: 59) notes that being coerced is intrinsically unpleasant. Tocqueville shares with Marx, Weber, Durkheim, and the other great macro-social theorists a concern for freedom, particularly in the modern Western world. People live in their respective communities; whether identified as integration, solidarity, or moral or value consensus, social scientists are centrally concerned with community; and analysis of its nature, sources, and consequences is a distinctive concern of sociologists. Power is the distinctive concern of political scientists. Many political theorists, and many social theorists as well, view society as a hierarchically structured system of power. Certainly this is true of those in the conflict tradition of Machiavelli, Hobbes, Marx, and Weber (Collins, 1978; 1975; 56-81). Tocqueville is centrally concerned with the two decisive dimensions of social power, its concentration and legitimacy.

Tocqueville's theory is one of freedom-tyranny, community-egoism, decentralized-centralized administration, and authority-force. It links freedom to balanced, legitimate power. Maximizing the opportunity to do so, such power encourages people to pursue their interest energetically. His theory of community asserts that a free people's pursuit of their interests brings them into contact, which causes them to become concerned about one another. Through contact they develop social structures that help them realize their interests, including the perpetuation of freedom. Decentralized administration encourages people to act energetically and organize, which in turn promotes both community and freedom. His theory of authority holds that freedom and community encourage government to use its authority in ways, for example, to help people to realize their interests, which perpetuate that authority. Tocqueville's theory is a theory of the relations between or among any two or three of these variables. For instance, in the title of a work indebted to Tocqueville, it is a theory of *Community and Power* (Nisbet, 1962). Most inclusively it is a theory of the relations among all four variables. Tocqueville's theory not only deals with basic phenomena but explains them in terms of their mutual relations.

Tocqueville's work illustrates the risks of ranging widely. Inclusiveness can undermine the appearance of theoretical integration. Tocqueville's insightfulness is often lauded even as his theoretical contributions are denied. Identification of the theoretical core of his work permits us to recognize that he achieves both range and integration. Tocqueville does not treat this core as a closed, self-contained system. Rather, he feels that the value of each core variable affects and is affected by other variables, both those in the core itself and many outside it. For example, in reducing egoism, individualism, and materialism, religion promotes community and freedom. Or, to take a different kind of variable, by reducing pressures for centralization geographic isolation promotes freedom. Tocqueville's approach gives his theory the strength of extension, while avoiding its dangers, and the strength of intension, while avoiding an overly narrow focus that ignores too many important factors. On the one hand, his analysis incorporates an array of factors and seems to omit nothing vital. But to the extent that it does—certainly its contemporary development is likely to entail inclusion of factors Tocqueville slighted—additional variables can readily be introduced, as Tocqueville himself does (by establishing their relations with his core variables). On the other hand, Tocqueville's theoretical core provides focus, continuity, manageability, and a framework for analyzing innumerable additional variables. Tocqueville's theory is both manageable and inclusive, both focused and extensive. He resolves the tension between intension and extension.

We cannot know the form of future theory as social scientists develop increasingly viable theoretical perspectives. Nonetheless, many social scientists will find aspects of Tocqueville's theory refreshing. He avoids monocausality, determinism, reductionism, and reification. Recognizing the importance of various kinds of factors, Tocqueville typically viewed them as existing in a state of partial autonomy coupled with reciprocal influence. He asserts the importance of both structural and social psychological factors, of the characteristic personality types of individuals in given groups, classes, and nations (national character), and both ideas and interests. He is sensitive to the importance of class, status, and political power and of their reciprocal relations.

We may seek the sources of Tocqueville's theoretical persuasiveness. Are we convinced for the right reasons and what are the instructive aspects of his approach? Much of Tocqueville's persuasiveness derives from the power of elegant writing. A second element is the intuitive appeal of his theory. Tocqueville's explanations of behavior and institutions are believable because they are consistent with what we read in history or see in contemporary society and our everyday lives. Rather than reifying institutions or historical forces, he portrays these as the sum of the meaningful and understandable actions of individual people under given circumstances. He does not portray individuals as driven by subterranean or mysterious factors. Rather, his theory incorporates reasonable assumptions about social behavior and power. Even while constrained by circumstances people retain some freedom. People like freedom. Ideas are important. People pursue their own ideal and material interests as they define them and also seek to further their social, economic, and political interests. Interaction generates mutual concern. People are willing to use their power to coerce other people. Unbalanced power becomes first arbitrary and ultimately tyrannical. The way to prevent this is to oppose one power with another.

Nothing is more subject to debate than the reasonableness of theoretical assumptions. Congruence with the evidence is a potentially more objective test of a theory. One of Tocqueville's great strengths is his comparative-historical approach, an approach he not incidentally shares with many other important social scientists. Born just sixteen years after the outbreak of the French Revolution, Tocqueville lived during a period of rapid transition from aristocratic to democratic society. He was concerned with each and with their comparison. Coming from an aristocratic family that had suffered at the hands of the Revolution—some of his ancestors were killed and only the ninth Thermidor saved his imprisoned parents from execution—Tocqueville held many aristocratic values. He felt great emotion at a family gathering when his mother sang a song about Louis XVI. His loyalty to the monarchy and affection for French kings caused him to cry when he (1970: 65n) saw Charles X's carriages departing Versailles after that king was deposed by Louis-Phillippe. If family, emotion, and values linked him to aristocratic society, his concern to promote freedom directed his attention to democratic society. This interest coupled with a conjunction of political and personal circumstances encouraged a journey to

America that he otherwise would probably not have undertaken. This trip gave him firsthand exposure to the most democratic country in the world, and, presumably, further stimulated his interest in democracy and use of a comparative approach.

Analyzing aristocratic and democratic society as contrasting and in some ways opposite—the former is defined by inequality, the latter by equality—ideal types, Tocqueville shows that his theory of freedom applies equally to each. However theoretically decisive, this demonstration is just one instance of Tocqueville's comparative-historical approach. He writes about a number of countries, including Algeria, Canada, Germany, India, Ireland, Mexico, and Switzerland. He focuses particularly on France, the United States, and England. It is hard to think of another author who so carefullly compares three nations over such long periods of their history. Tocqueville's ability to demonstrate that the relationships he postulates hold in both aristocratic and democratic societies and in the period of transition from the former to the latter, in given countries over the centuries (for example, in France from feudal times to Tocqueville's day), in old (England) and new (United States, Canada) societies, and in societies differing in history, culture, and geography does much to demonstrate his theory's validity.

Nonscientific values influence scientists' selection of subject matter. Commitment to freedom heightens interest in Tocqueville's theory. In addition, the response to theories is influenced by the degree to which a theory says what scientists want to hear. Tocqueville explains how the values of modern, liberal, democratic society can be realized. These same values will foster reservations about a theory that states that people must choose between freedom and equality or justice or settle for a trade-off between equality and prosperity. The scientific merits of such a theory might make it attractive. However, the depressing assertion that the fulfillment of some values precludes the fulfillment of others will dispose scientists to search for a theory that does not have this drawback or, even better, asserts that the realization of one value promotes fulfillment of others. Tocqueville's is such a theory. He explains how freedom is causally associated with the good, tyranny with the bad.

This is not to say that Tocqueville bases his theory on unrealistically postive assumptions about human nature, social structures, or history. A realist and, toward the end of his life, often profoundly pessimistic about the future of freedom in France, Tocqueville was no Pollyanna offering pie in the sky. He felt that, in general, people were neither very good nor very bad. His assumptions about human nature, interests, power, and domination contain the realpolitik common to conflict theorists. His recognition of the unfavorable aspects of human nature and social structures fueled his concern to state the conditions that would make individuals and social structures not ideal but as good as they could be.

Comparing aristocratic and democratic society, he regretted the losses inherent in the great transformation. However, within the limits of what is possible in egalitarian society, as the antidote to its distinctive vices, freedom makes this society as good as it can be. If egalitarianism engenders materialism, individualism, and a lack of concern with the public good, and reduces national greatness, freedom promotes community, morality, political involvement, social and economic prosperity, and individual and national greatness. Those raised in and imbued with the values of democratic society will experience the loss of aristocratic values less acutely and will evaluate many features of egalitarian society more positively than did Tocqueville. As described by Tocqueville free democratic society will appear even better to its products than it did to Tocqueville himself.

For Tocqueville choosing between aristocratic and democratic society creates a dilemma because each has distinctive strengths and weaknesses. His assertion that the realization of some values undercuts the realization of others occurs in the context of the aristocratic-democratic society comparison. His account of liberal democratic society promises as much as we, products of that society, could hope for. Its basis in the assumptions of conflict theory is reassuring in that such assumptions appear founded not in wishful thinking but in a realistic, hardheaded approach to the world. It asserts that the values basic to modern, liberal democratic society—freedom, community, morality, justice, authority, prosperity, and national greatness—are mutually causative and define a configuration. It further asserts that all these can be combined with equality. The promise of Tocqueville's theory commands attention. Lest it seduce us by telling us what we want to hear, this promise should reinforce the concern we feel to evaluate any scientific theory critically.

Tocqueville employs a class, status, political power model of society the viability of which is demonstrated not only in Tocqueville but equally (and sometimes more consciously) in Weber and in the work of the many contemporary analysts who continue to employ it. Collapsing class and status into society, we derive Tocqueville's state and society model which, again, has proved useful to Weber and many others. In contrast to Marx who often sees the state as an outgrowth of society's economic structure, Collins (1975:58) argues for the analytic primacy of the coercive violence controlled by the state. Rather than asserting the primacy of either state or society, Tocqueville is ever concerned with both and their relations. He is particularly concerned that the state's power not overwhelm that of society. Society must be strong, especially as manifested in community and strong, multiple centers of power. The state must lack the structural means, centralized administration, to dominate the society. Tocqueville analyzes the reciprocally causative relations between community and decentralized administration. He fears that the power of a monolithic state, unchecked by power diffused throughout society, will become a tyrannical power dominating a defenseless society.

Famous for his prescience, Tocqueville identifies the demand for equality as the dominant force in the modern world. Collectively, the trends produced by the demand for equality in the major spheres of life—social, economic, political, legal, administrative, educational, and familial—and in major opportunity structures constitute what some analysts regard as the fundamental change in contemporary society. The demand for equality spreads to both larger and smaller social structures. Tocqueville (1969:584-589) notes how egalitarian mores affect familial relations. In international relations the demand for equality is increasingly pressed by smaller, weaker nations. Because, as Tocqueville recognizes, there may be little community at this level, these relations are often mediated in terms of force, not authority. Whatever their ideological legitimacy, the demands by the weaker nations for greater equality are often left unmet.

If more and more groups are fired by the demand for greater equality, Tocqueville emphasizes that such demands meet with varying resistance by others, including those in power. The result is a history of ebb and flow as different groups meet with varying and ever changing success. Many factors, including the date of its inception, the prevalence of different ideologies, and the relative size, unity, and strength of and alignments among the major actors in the drama—the working class, the middle class, the upper class, and the state—affect the relative development of the welfare state, which is much more highly developed in some places such as Scandinavia than in others, for example, the United States. If the long-term trend is toward expansion, in the short run its development may be anything but linear. Within a given country some groups may be more successful in pressing their demands for equality than other groups and may achieve greater equality in some areas than in others. The civil rights movement largely achieved its original demands; and, indeed, its success eventually undermined the movement's strength. However, these gains were not accompanied by greater overall black economic equality. A few blacks have moved into higher positions from which they were previously excluded. However, the median black household income as a percentage of that of whites was less in 1979 (58.9%) than in 1970 (60.9%) (U.S. Bureau of the Census, 1981: 432). And, as Tocqueville recognizes, demands for equality may produce unintended effects. Currently, in the United States a higher proportion of women than men graduate from high school and the two sexes are virtually even in the proportions receiving bachelor's degrees (Stockard and Johnson, 1980: 68). However, among year-round, full-time workers, women's wages relative to men's actually declined from 1960 to 1977 (Stockard and Johnson, 1980: 30-31). Furthermore, many middle-class American women have found that greater economic equality in the form of paid jobs has not been accompanied by a commensurate increase in equality in the division of household labor. Women have simply added such jobs to their household responsibilities. The result has been decreased rather than increased sexual equality in the total work load of these women compared to that of their partners.

Tocqueville notes that many things contributed to the massive change from aristocratic to democratic society. Obviously, however, there were powerful opposing forces as well. If the equality-producing factors had encountered no resistance, the democratic revolution would hardly have lasted 700 years by Tocqueville's time, nor would Tocqueville have predicted that it would continue into the foreseeable future. Tocqueville assumed that those with power would seek to increase their advantages. Even as numerous sources of privilege were attacked, Tocqueville identified certain economic changes—particularly the growth of the market and the development of large-scale manufacturing—as increasingly important sources of inequality. Just as the tension between the demand for equality and the inequality of existing institutions fired the emotions leading to the French Revolution, so also Tocqueville asserted the revolutionary potential created by the tension between economic inequality and democratic society's ever-growing demand for equality. Though embedded in different analyses, and though one saw inequality and the other equality as the dominant trend of modern society, Marx and Tocqueville converge in believing that the greater the inequality and polarization generated by the market and industry, the more likely are turmoil and even revolution.

Democratic governments seek to promote equality. Products of their age, they are ideologically committed to the equality of citizens, that is, vis-à-vis each other. By promoting equality a government meets the people's demands, which in turn promotes its authority. Permitting the government to treat all equally, equality increases administrative rationalization and power. In equalizing its citizenry, a government reduces, levels, and renders all equally subordinate to itself. Finally, equality promotes the materialism and individualism that atomizes the people. Divided, weak, and free to pursue their materialistic goals, the citizens seldom actively seek to oppose the government. Even should they desire to do so, they lack the means—that is, the power of organization.

Tocqueville's comparative approach takes into account the differences among nations and treats each as a unique case. I apply his perspectives to the country analyzed in his longest book. In the United States, from Tocqueville's time to the present, the power of larger governments has grown relative to and often at the expense of smaller, more local governments. Most important, the federal government has expanded greatly. This growth in power has taken place in the name of the people's interest, as well as the national interest. Technological advances reduce America's relative immunity from the military threat of foreign nations that, together with numerous other factors, has contributed to its greatly increased involvement in the international political economy. One consequence has been a vast growth in the military establishment. Itself constituting centralization, this growth has been accompanied by the additional centralization designed to support it. The three demands characteristic of a free democratic society—equality, freedom, and prosperity—have engendered further centralization.

The history of the United States can be seen as the interplay among these three demands and state power. The welfare state has grown in response to increasing demands for a more extensive bundle of rights. More and more groups have pressed their demands for greater equality. The privileges of one group are often experienced by other groups as reductions of their freedom. Thus demands may be presented for greater freedom or greater equality or both. The impact of these demands on the government and its use of power has produced contrary results. Increased centralization has both increased and decreased equality, community, authority, and freedom. The increased centralization and power that has enabled the government to promote equality also increases the power differential between itself and its citizens. The demands for equality increase both equality and inequality.

The federal government has increased its authority by meeting the people's demands for equality and freedom. Its growth, bureaucratization, and centralization of administration make the government appear as an ever more distant, impervious, and potentially imperial power to a people who believe in their sovereignty and who judge government by its responsiveness to their needs. Centralization increases the government's ability to act in arbitrary ways that, insofar as people are powerless to change them, will be judged increasingly as tyrannical, however inspired by egalitarian, humanitarian, or other basic values of democratic society.

In reducing its citizens' control over their own lives, particularly their everyday lives at the local level, centralization reduces their reason to cooperate in pursuit of their interests. Excluding contacts among a circle of family and friends or those in the economic sphere, people have less contact with one another. They are less concerned about one another and are less organized to control their own lives and to promote their own interests including that of protecting their own freedom. However, if centralization decreases community it also increases it. Policies enforced by a centralized administration may increase the freedom of the poor and minority groups and produce a more egalitarian opportunity structure. Many who were previously excluded enter or at last seek to enter the mainstream. Like the change from aristocratic to democratic society, increased freedom gives more people reason to attempt, individually and collectively, to take advantage energetically of the widespread opportunities to seek to realize the material and other promises of democratic society.

Finally, and most important, the national government's power both increases and reduces freedom. Centralization of government—central (national) direction of matters of national interest—is necessary for national survival and to promote varied national interests, including that of freedom itself, for example, the civil rights legislation of the 1960s. Yet, centralization of administration—regulations, restrictions, and administrative guidelines affecting matters of local interest—reduce diversity, promote uniformity, override local authority, and otherwise reduce freedom.

Although there are many ways to promote freedom, prudence directs concerned citizens and lawmakers to channel their necessarily limited influence in directions most likely to be fruitful. Tocqueville opposed the growth of centralization in France. Emphasizing the freedom-reducing aspects of its growth, contemporary conservatives advocate reduced government (although revealing their kinship with nonconservatives, they also encourage government intervention favorable to their interests). Against at least those conservatives who too freely equate the market with freedom, Tocqueville assumes that unopposed concentrations of power, whether social, political, or economic, are the source of tyranny. In aristocratic society the aristocracy exercised what by the standards of liberal, democratic society was tyrannical power over the peasants and others subject to their jurisdiction. Similarly, in capitalist society economic inequalities not only make for unequal, unfair bargaining between economic giants and individual workers, but can debase workers forced to submit to the tyrannical working conditions sometimes imposed by those giants. Furthermore, Tocqueville warns that failure to redress these dehumanizing inequalities will produce the turmoil and revolution that he and conservatives alike dislike and that undermine freedom. Contemporary liberals argue for more government to promote freedom by reducing market and other inequalities in power. Against these liberals Tocqueville warns of a centralized administration's threat to freedom. Though one group argues for reduced and the other for increased government—conservatives seeking freedom in reduced government and in a society strong enough to withstand any governmental threat to freedom, liberals seeking freedom in a government strong enough to control society's and especially the economy's threat to freedom—each, of course, does so in the name of freedom. The overall impact of increased governmental power in the United States has been mixed. Consequently, the debate between liberals and conservatives continues.

Noting that people in opposite camps found support in his work, Tocqueville complained that in selecting only those portions that agreed with their own position they failed to consider his work as a whole and did not understand his position. Today we have no reason to reject Tocqueville's observation, but to them we may add his own analysis of the French Revolution. In some ways, particularly by eliminating privilege, reducing inequality, and developing new bases of legitimacy, the French Revolution promoted liberty. At the same time, and in the name of liberty, the revolution increased the centralization Tocqueville saw as the main threat to France's freedom. Similarly, government bureaucratization and the growth of the welfare state in Western Europe and its offshoots have promoted liberty. However, these same development can undermine community and freedom.

Like equality, liberty and community are inclusive, multifaceted phenomena. Each can grow in some ways while being threatened or reduced in others. This is one way in which Tocqueville's theory needs development. While recognizing that each of his major concepts was multidimensional, Tocqueville often treated each in a global, unitary fashion. Doing so helped him to state a theory of freedom. Contemporary development of his theory requires identification of the dimensions of each major concept and specification of the relations of these dimensions with each other and the variables in his theory.

Tocqueville offers a compelling theory of authority, decentralization of administration, community, and above all, freedom. When in power contemporary enemies of freedom often act as if they have a practical knowledge of his theory. Clothing their tryanny in the institutional trappings and rhetoric of liberty, they assert the sovereignty of the people and claim to represent their will and promote their interests. Reflecting the widespread love of liberty, they seek it for themselves while denying it to others. I reiterate Tocqueville's hope that those who share his commitments will find in his theory lessons useful in promoting freedom. I also hope that the power and promise of his theory will inspire efforts to develop it further.

References

Alexander, J. C. (1982) Theoretical Logic in Sociology, Vol. 1: Positivism, Presuppositions, and Current Controversies. Berkeley: University of California Press.

Almond, G. A. (1950) The American People and Foreign Policy. New York: Harcourt Brace Jovanovich.

Aron, R. (1965) Main Currents in Sociological Thought, Vol. 1: Montesquieu/Comte/Marx/Tocqueville/The Sociologists and the Revolution of 1848 (R. Howard and H. Weaver, trans.). New York: Basic Books.

———(1966) "Social class, political class, ruling class," pp. 201-210 in R. Bendix and S. M. Lipset (eds.) Class, Status, and Power: Social Stratification in Comparative Perspective. New York: Free Press.

———(1967) Main Currents in Sociological Thought, Vol. 2: Durkheim/Pareto/Weber (R. Howard and H. Weaver, trans.). New York: Basic Books.

———(1968) Progress and Disillusion. New York: Praeger.

Avineri, S. (1968) The Social and Political Thought of Karl Marx. Cambridge: Cambridge University Press.

Baker, R. (1976) "Off the top of de Tocq." New York Times (November 23): 33.

Baltzell, E. D. (1964) The Protestant Establishment: Aristocracy and Caste in America. New York: Random House.

———(1979) Puritan Boston and Quaker Philadelphia: Two Protestant Ethics and the Spirit of Class Authority and Leadership. New York: Free Press.

Banks, A. S. (1971) Cross-Polity Time-Series Data. Cambridge: MIT Press.

Barnes, H. E. [ed.] (1948) An Introduction to the History of Sociology. Chicago: University of Chicago Press.

Barnes, H. E. and H. Becker (1938) Social Thought From Lore to Science, Vol. 1: A History and Interpretation of Man's Ideas about Life with His Fellows. Boston: Heath.

Beaumont, G. de and A. de Tocqueville (1964) On the Penitentiary System in the United States and Its Application in France (1833). Carbondale: Southern Illinois University Press.

Bell, D (1976) The Coming of Post-Industrial Society. New York: Basic Books.

Bellah, R. N. (1970) Beyond Belief. New York: Harper & Row.

Beloff, M. (1962) The Age of Absolutism 1660-1815. New York: Harper Torchbooks.

Bendix, R. (1962) Max Weber: An Intellectual Portrait. Garden City, NY: Doubleday.

———(1977) Nation-Building and Citizenship. Studies of Our Changing Social Order. Berkeley: University of California Press.

———(1978) Kings or People: Power and the Mandate to Rule. Berkeley: University of California Press.

Berlin, I. (1965) "The thought of de Tocqueville" (review of The Social and Political Thought of Alexis de Tocqueville, by J. Lively). History 50: 199-206.

Bluhm, W. (1978) Theories of the Political System: Classics of Political Thought and Modern Political Analysis. Englewood Cliffs, NJ: Prentice-Hall.

Boesche, R. C. (1981) "The strange liberalism of Alexis de Tocqueville." History of Political Thought 2: 495-524.

Boorstin, D. J. (1953) The Genius of American Politics. Chicago: Phoenix.

Brogan, H. (1973) Tocqueville. London: Collins/Fontana.

Byrce, J. (1887) "The predictions of Hamilton and DeTocqueville." Herbert B. Adams (ed.), Johns Hopkins University Studies in Historical and Political Science, Vol. 5, Baltimore: Johns Hopkins University Press.

Collins, R. (1968) "A comparative approach to political sociology," pp. 42-67 in R. Bendix et al. (eds.) State and Society: A Reader in Comparative Political Sociology. Boston: Little, Brown.

———(1975) Conflict Sociology: Toward an Explanatory Science. New York: Academic.

———(1978) "The empirical validity of the conflict tradition," pp. 168-89 in A. Wells (ed.) Contemporary Sociological Theories. Santa Monica, CA: Goodyear.

Collins, R. and M. Makowsky (1978) The Discovery of Society. New York: Random House.

Commager, H. S. (1946) "Introduction," pp. vii-xxiii in Henry Steele Commager (ed.) Democracy in America by Alexis de Tocqueville. (H. Reeve, trans.) London: Oxford University Press.

———(1950) The American Mind: An Interpretation of American Thought and Character Since the 1880's. New Haven, CT: Yale University Press.

Coser, L. A. (1977) Masters of Sociological Thought: Ideas in Historical and Social Context. New York: Harcourt Brace Jovanovich.

Cuzzort, R. P. and E. W. King (1980) Twentieth Century Social Thought. New York: Holt, Rinehart & Winston.

Dahl, R. A. (1976) Democracy in the United States: Promise and Performance. Chicago: Rand McNally.

Dahrendorf, R. (1961) "Democracy without liberty: an essay on the politics of other-directed man," pp. 175-206 in S. M. Lipset and L. Lowenthal (eds.) Culture and Social Character: The Work of David Riesman Reviewed. New York: Free Press.

Davies, J. C. (1962) "Toward a theory of revolution." American Sociological Review 27: 5-19.

Demerath, N. J., III and R. A. Peterson [eds.] (1967) System, Change, and Conflict: A Reader on Contemporary Sociological Theory and the Debate Over Functionalism. New York: Free Press.

Drescher, S. (1964a) Tocqueville and England. Cambridge, MA: Harvard University Press.

———(1964b) "Tocqueville's two democracies." Journal of the History of Ideas 25: 201-216.

———(1968a) Dilemmas of Democracy: Tocqueville and Modernization. University of Pittsburgh Press.

———(1968b) "Introduction," pp. ix-xx in S. Drescher (ed.) Tocqueville and Beaumont on Social Reform. New York: Harper Torchbooks.

———(1980) "Tocqueville, Alexis de." New Encyclopedia Britannica. 18: 468-471.

Durkheim, E. (1951) Suicide (G. Simpson, ed., J. A. Spaulding and G. Simpson, trans.) (1897). New York: Free Press.

———(1956) Education and Sociology (S. D. Fox, trans.) (1922). New York: Free Press.

———(1958) Professional Ethics and Civic Morals (C. Brookfield, trans.) (1950). New York: Free Press.

———(1960) The Division of Labor in Society (G. Simpson, trans.) (1893). New York: Free Press.

———(1961) Moral Education (E. K. Wilson and H. Schnurer, trans.) (1925). New York: Free Press.

———(1964) The Rules of Sociological Method (S. A. Solovay and J. H. Mueller, trans.) (1895). New York: Free Press.

———(1965) The Elementary Forms of the Religious Life (J. W. Swain, trans.) (1912). New York: Free Press.

———(1973a) "Individualism and the intellectuals" (1898), pp. 43-57 in R. N. Bellah (ed.) Emile Durkheim on Mortality and Society: Selected Writings. Chicago: University of Chicago Press.

———(1973b) "The dualism of human nature and its social conditions" (1914), pp. 149-163 in R. N. Bellah (ed.) Emile Durkheim on Morality and Society: Selected Writings. Chicago: University of Chicago Press.

———(1974) Sociology and Philosophy (D. F. Pocock, trans.) (1924). New York: Free Press.

Ebenstein, W. (1957) Political Thought in Perspective. New York: McGraw-Hill.

———(1969) Great Political Thinkers: Plato to the Present. New York: Holt, Rinehart & Winston.

Eberts, P. R. and R. A. Witton (1970) "Recall from anecdote: Alexis de Tocqueville and the morphogenesis of America." American Sociological Review 35: 1081-1097.

Faris, R.E.L. [ed.] (1964) Handbook of Modern Sociology. Chicago: Rand McNally.

Fenton, S. with R. Reiner and I. Hamnett (1984) Durkheim and Modern Sociology. Cambridge: Cambridge University Press.

Furet, F. (1981) Interpreting the French Revolution (E. Forster, trans.). Cambridge: Cambridge University Press.

Gargan, E. T. (1955) Alexis de Tocqueville: The Critical Years, 1848-1851. Washington, DC: Catholic University of America Press.

———(1959) "Some problems in Tocqueville scholarship." Mid-America 41: 3-26.

———(1962) "The formation of Tocqueville's historical thought." Review of Politics 24: 48-61.

———(1963) "Tocqueville and the problem of historical prognosis." American Historical Review 68: 332-345.

———(1965) De Tocqueville. New York: Hillary House.

Germino, D. (1972) Modern Western Political Thought: Machiavelli to Marx. Chicago: Rand McNally.

Gibbs, J. P. (1972) Sociological Theory Construction. Hinsdale, ILL: Dryden.

Giddens, A. (1971) Capitalism and Modern Social Theory. London: Cambridge University Press.

Goldstein, D. S. (1975) Trial of Faith: Religion and Politics in Tocqueville's Thought. New York: Elsevier.

Halebsky, S. (1976) Mass Society and Political Conflict. Cambridge: Cambridge University Press.

Hartz, L. (1955) The Liberal Tradition in America. New York: Harcourt Brace Jovanovich.

Herberg, W. (1960) Protestant-Catholic-Jew. Garden City, NY: Doubleday.

Herr, R. (1962) Tocqueville and the Old Regime. Princeton, NJ: Princeton University Press.

Hoffman, S. (1982) "Year one." New York Review of Books 29 (August 12): 37-43.

Horowitz, I. L. (1967) "Consensus, conflict and co-operation," pp. 265-279 in N. J. Demerath III and R. A. Peterson (eds.) System, Change, and Conflict: A Reader on Contemporary Sociological Theory and the Debate over Functionalism. New York: Free Press.

Huntington, S. P. (1968) Political Order in Changing Societies. New Haven, CT: Yale University Press.

Inkeles, A. (1979) "Continuity and change in the American national character," pp. 389-416 in S. M. Lipset (ed.) The Third Century: America as a Post-Industrial Society. Stanford, CA: Hoover Institution Press.

Johnson, D. P. (1981) Sociological Theory: Classical Founders and Contemporary Perpectives. New York: John Wiley.

Jones, R. A. and S. Kronus (1976) "Professional sociologists and the history of sociology: a survey of recent opinion." Journal of the History of the Behavioral Sciences 12: 3-13.

Kornhauser, W. (1959) The Politics of Mass Society. New York: Free Press.

Lenski, G. E. (1966) Power and Privilege: A Theory of Social Stratification. New York: McGraw-Hill.

———and J. Lenski (1978) Human Societies. New York: McGraw-Hill.

Lerner, M. (1966) "Introduction: Tocqueville and America," pp. xxv-lxxxiii in J. P. Mayer and M. Lerner (eds.) Democracy in America by Alexis de Tocqueville (G. Lawrence, trans.). New York: Harper & Row.

Lipset, S. (1963) Political Man: The Social Bases of Politics. Garden City, NY: Doubleday.

———M. A. Trow, and J. S. Coleman (1956) Union Democracy. New York: Free Press.

Lively, J. (1962) The Social and Political Thought of Alexis de Tocqueville. Oxford: Clarendon Press.

Lukacs, J. (1968) "Introduction," pp. 1-28 in Alexis de Tocqueville, "The European Revolution" and Correspondence with Gobineau (J. Lukacs, ed. and trans.). Gloucester, MA: Peter Smith.

———(1982) "Alexis de Tocqueville: a historical appreciation." Literature of Liberty 5: 7-42.

Lukes, S. (1972) Emile Durkheim: His Life and Work. New York: Harper & Row.

Mannheim, K. (1936) Ideology and Utopia. New York: Harvest.

Marshall, L. L. and S. Drescher (1968) "American historians and Tocqueville's 'Democracy.'" Journal of American History 55: 512-532.

Martindale, D. (1960) The Nature and Types of Sociological Theory. Boston: Houghton Mifflin.

———(1981) The Nature and Types of Sociological Theory. Boston: Houghton Mifflin.

Marx, K. (1977) Karl Marx: Selected Writings (D. McLellan, ed.). Oxford: Oxford University Press.

———and F. Engels (1972) The Marx-Engels Reader (R. C. Tucker, ed.). New York: Norton.

———(1978) The Marx-Engels Reader (2nd ed., R. C. Tucker, ed.). New York: Norton.

Masaryk, T. G. (1970) Suicide and the Meaning of Civilization. (W. B. Weist and R. G. Batson, trans.) (1881). Chicago: University of Chicago Press.

Mayer, J. P. (1966a) Alexis de Tocqueville (1939). Gloucester, MA: Peter Smith.

———(1966b) "Foreword," pp. vii-ix in J. P. Mayer and M. Lerner (eds.) Democracy in America by Alexis de Tocqueville (G. Lawrence, trans.) New York: Harper & Row.

Merton, R. K. (1957) Social Theory and Structure. New York: Free Press.

Meyers, M. (1957) The Jacksonian Persuasion: Politics and Belief. Stanford, CA: Stanford University Press.

Michels, R. (1959) Political Parties. (E. Paul and C. Paul, trans.) (1915). New York: Dover.

Mill, J. S. (1884) A System of Logic. London: Longmans, Green.

———(1962) "Tocqueville on democracy in America (Vol. II)" (1840), pp. 230-287 in G. Himmelfarb (ed.) Essays on Politics and Culture. Garden City, NY: Doubleday.

Mills, C. W. (1959) The Power Elite. New York: Galaxy.

Moore, B., Jr. (1966) Social Origins of Dictatorship and Democracy: Lord and Peasant in the Making of the Modern World. Boston: Beacon.

Nef, J. (1963) "Truth, belief, and civilization: Tocqueville and Gobineau." Review of Politics 25: 460-482.

Nisbet, R. A. (1962) Community and Power. New York: Galaxy.

———(1966) The Sociological Tradition. New York: Basic Books.

———(1968) "Tocqueville, Alexis de," pp. 90-95 in D. L. Sills (ed.) International Encyclopedia of the Social Sciences. New York: Macmillan.

———(1974) The Sociology of Emile Durkheim. New York: Oxford University Press.

———(1975) Twilight of Authority. New York: Oxford University Press.

———(1977) "Many Tocquevilles." American Scholar 46: 59-75.

Palmer, R. R. (1959) The Age of the Democratic Revolution: A Political History of Europe and America, 1760-1800, Vol. 1: The Challenge. Princeton, NJ: Princeton University Press.

———(1964) The Age of the Democratic Revolution: A Political History of Europe and America, 1760-1800, Vol. 2: The Struggle. Princeton, NJ: Princeton University Press.

Park, R. E. and E. W. Burgess (1969) Introduction to the Science of Sociology (1921). Chicago: University of Chicago Press.

Parsons, T. (1954) Essays in Sociological Theory. New York: Free Press.

———(1966) Societies: Evolutionary and Comparative Perspectives. Englewood Cliffs, NJ: Prentice-Hall.

———(1967) Review symposium on Robert A. Nisbet. "The sociological tradition." American Sociological Review 32: 640-643.

———(1968) The Structure of Social Action, Vol. 1: Marshall, Pareto, Durkheim (1937). New York: Free Press.

———(1971) The System of Modern Societies. Englewood Cliffs: Prentice-Hall.

Pessen, E. (1978) Jacksonian America: Society, Personality, and Politics. Homewood IL: Dorsey.

———(1979) "On a recent cliometric attempt to resurrect the myth of antebellum egalitarianism." Social Science History 3: 208-227.

———(1982) "Social structure and politics in American history." American Historical Review 87: 1290-1325.

Pierson, G. W. (1938) Tocqueville and Beaumont in America. New York: Oxford.

———(1969) Tocqueville in America (abridged by D. C. Lunt, from Tocqueville and Beaumont in America). Gloucester, MA: Peter Smith.

———(1980) "Foreword," pp xv-xix in J. T. Schleifer, The Making of Tocqueville's Democracy in America. Chapel Hill: University of North Carolina Press.

Piven, F. F. and R. A. Cloward (1979) Poor People's Movements: Why They Succeed, How They Fail. New York: Vintage.

Poggi, G. (1972) Images of Society: Essays on the Sociological Theories of Tocqueville, Marx, and Durkheim. Stanford, CA: Stanford University Press.

Potter, D. M. (1954) People of Plenty. Chicago: University of Chicago Press.

Probst, G. E. [ed.] (1962) The Happy Republic: A Reader in Tocqueville's America. New York: Harper Torchbooks.

Radcliffe-Brown, A. R. (1952) Structure and Function in Primitive Society. London: Cohen & West.

Redier, A. (1925) Comme Disait Monsieur de Tocqueville. Paris: Perrin.

Rhea, B. [ed.] (1981) The Future of the Sociological Classics. London: George Allen & Unwin.

Richter, M. (1958) "A debate on race: the Tocqueville-Gobineau correspondence." Commentary 25: 151-160.

————(1963) "Tocqueville on Algeria." Review of Politics 25: 362-398.

————(1967) "Tocqueville's contributions to the theory of revolution," pp. 75-121 in C. J. Friedrich (ed.) Revolution. Nomos VIII. New York: Atherton.

————(1969) "Comparative political analysis in Montesquieu and Tocqueville." Comparative Politics 1: 129-160.

————(1970) "The uses of theory: Tocqueville's adaptation of Montesquieu," pp. 74-102 in M. Richter (ed.) Essays in Theory and History. Cambridge: Harvard University Press.

Riesman, D. in collaboration with R. Denney and N. Glazer (1950) The Lonely Crowd: A Study of the Changing American Character. New Haven, CT: Yale University Press.

Ritzer, G. (1983) Sociological Theory. New York: Knopf.

Rossides, D. W. (1978) The History and Nature of Sociological Theory. Boston: Houghton Mifflin.

Sabine, G. H. (1961) A History of Political Theory. New York: Holt, Rinehart & Winston.

Salomon, A. (1960) "Tocqueville, 1959." Social Research 27: 449-470.

————(1962) In Praise of Enlightenment. Cleveland, OH: Meridian.

Schapiro, J. S. (1942) "Alexis de Tocqueville, pioneer of democratic liberalism in France." Political Science Quarterly 57: 545-563.

Schleifer, J. T. (1980) The Making of Tocqueville's Democracy in America. Chapel Hill: University of North Carolina Press.

Shils, E. (1961) "Epilogue: the calling of sociology," pp. 1403-1448 in T. Parsons et al. (eds.) Theories of Society, Vol. 2. New York: Free Press.

Sibley, M. Q. (1970) Political Ideas and Ideologies: A History of Political Thought. New York: Harper & Row.

Simmel, G. (1950) The Sociology of Georg Simmel (K. H. Wolff, ed. and trans.). New York: Free Press.

Skocpol, T. (1979) States and Social Revolutions: A Comparative Analysis of France, Russia, and China. Cambridge: Cambridge University Press.

Smelser, N. J. (1976) Comparative Methods in the Social Sciences. Englewood Cliffs, NJ: Prentice-Hall.

————and R. S. Warner (1976) Sociological Theory: Historical and Formal. Morristown, NJ: General Learning Press.

Smith, C. and A. Freedman (1972) Voluntary Associations: Perspectives on the Literature. Cambridge, MA: Harvard University Press.

Smith, P. (1981) The Nation Comes of Age: A People's History of the Ante-Bellum Years, Vol. 4. New York: McGraw-Hill.

Sorokin, P. (1928) Contemporary Sociological Theories. New York: Harper & Row.

Spiller, R. E., W. Thorp, T. H. Johnson, H. S. Canby, R. M. Ludwig, and W. M. Gibson [eds.] (1974) Literary History of the United States: History. London: Macmillan.

Stinchcombe, A. L. (1968) Constructing Social Theories. New York: Harcourt Brace Jovanovich.

————(1978) Theoretical Methods in Social History. New York: Academic Press.

Stockyard, J. and M. M. Johnson (1980) Sex Roles: Sex Inequality and Sex Role Development. Englewood Cliffs, NJ: Prentice-Hall.

Stone, J. and S. Mennell (1980) "Introduction," pp. 1-46 in J. Stone and S. Mennell (eds.) Alexis de Tocqueville on Democracy, Revolution, and Society: Selected Writings. Chicago: University of Chicago Press.

Strauss, L. and J. Cropsey [eds.] (1972) History of Political Philosophy. Chicago: Rand McNally.

Takla, T. N. and W. Pope (1985) "The force imagery in Durkheim: the integration of theory, metatheory, and method." Sociological Theory.

Talmon, J. L. (1960a) The Origins of Totalitarian Democracy. New York: Praeger.

————(1960b) Political Messianism: The Romantic Phase. London: Secker & Warburg.

Taub, R. P. with D. L. Taub (1974) "Tocqueville and modern social science: an overview," pp. 3-19 in R. P. Taub with D. L. Taub (eds.) American Society in Tocqueville's Time and Today. Chicago: Rand McNally.

Tilton, T. A. (1979) "Alexis de Tocqueville and the political sociology of liberalism." Comparative Social Research 2: 263-287.

Timasheff, N. S. and G. A. Theodorson (1976) Sociological Theory: Its Nature and Growth. New York: Random House.

Tocqueville, A. de (1836) "Political and social condition of France" (J. S. Mill, trans.). London and Westminster Review: 75-92.

——(1861) Oeuvres et Correspondance Inedites (2 vols.) (G. de Beaumont, ed.). Paris: Freres.

——(1862) Memoir, Letters, and Remains of Alexis de Tocqueville (2 vols.) (trans. by the translator of "Napoleon's Correspondence with King Joseph"). Boston: Ticknor & Fields.

——(1945) Democracy in America (2 vols.) (H. Reeve, trans.) (1835, 1840). New York: Vintage.

——(1951) Oeuvres Complètes (J. P. Mayer, ed.). Paris: Gallimard.

——(1954) Correspondance Anglaise. Correspondance D'Alexis de Tocqueville Avec Henry Reeve et John Stuart Mill (Vol. 6, Pt. 1, Alexis de Tocqueville Oeuvres Complètes) (J. P. Mayer, ed.). Paris: Gallimard.

——(1955) The Old Regime and the French Revolution (S. Gilbert, trans.) (1856). Garden City, NY: Doubleday.

——(1966) Democracy in America (J. P. Mayer and M. Lerner, eds.; G. Lawrence, trans.) (1835, 1840). New York: Harper & Row.

——(1967) Correspondance d'Alexis de Tocqueville et de Gustave de Beaumont (Vol. 8, Pt. 3, Alexis de Tocqueville Oeuvres Complètes) (J. P. Mayer, ed.). Paris: Gallimard.

——(1968a) Journeys to England and Ireland (G. Lawrence and K. P. Mayer, trans.). Garden City, NY: Doubleday.

——(1968b) "The European Revolution" and Correspondence with Gobineau (J. Lukacs, ed. and trans.). Gloucester, MA: Peter Smith.

——(1969) Democracy in America (J. P. Mayer, ed.; G. Lawrence, trans.) (1835, 1840). Garden City, NY: Doubleday.

——(1970) Recollections (G. Lawrence, trans.) (1893). Garden City, NY: Doubleday.

——(1971) Journey to America (J. P. Mayer, ed.; G. Lawrence, trans.). Garden City, NY: Doubleday.

——(1980) Alexis de Tocqueville on Democracy, Revolution, and Society: Selected Writings (J. Stone and S. Mennell, eds.). Chicago: University of Chicago Press.

——and G. de Beaumont (1968) Tocqueville and Beaumont on Social Reform (S. Drescher, ed. and trans.). New York: Harper Torchbooks.

Tocqueville, A. de and N. W. Senior (1872) Correspondence and Conversations of Alexis de Tocqueville with Nassau William Senior from 1834 to 1859 (2 vols.). London: King.

Tonnies, F. (1957) Community and Society (C. P. Loomis, ed. and trans.) (1887). East Lansing: Michigan State University Press.

Turner, J. H. (1974) The Structure of Sociological Theory. Homewood, IL: Dorsey.

——(1978) The Structure of Sociological Theory (rev. ed.). Homewood, IL: Dorsey.

——and L. Beeghley (1981) The Emergence of Sociological Theory. Homewood, IL: Dorsey.

U.S. Bureau of the Census (1981) Statistical Abstract of the United States: 1981. Washington, DC: Government Printing Office.

Wach, J. (1946) "The role of religion in the social philosophy of Alexis de Tocqueville." Journal of the History of Ideas 7: 74-90.

Wallace, R. A. and A. Wolf (1980) Contemporary Sociological Theory. Englewood Cliffs, NJ: Prentice-Hall.

Wallace, W. L. (1971) The Logic of Science in Sociology. Chicago: Aldine/Atherton.

Warner, R. S. (1976) "Part one: sociological theory in historical context," pp. 1-133 in N. J. Smelser and R. S. Warner, Sociological Theory: Historical and Formal. Morristown, NJ: General Learning Press.

Warner, W. L. (1959) The Living and the Dead: A Study of the Symbolic Life of Americans. New Haven, CT: Yale University Press.

Weber, M. (1958a) From Max Weber: Essays in Sociology (H. H. Gerth and C. W. Mills, eds. and trans.). New York: Galaxy.

————(1958b) The Protestant Ethic and the Spirit of Capitalism (T. Parsons, trans.) (1904-1905). New York: Scribner's.

————(1961) General Economic History (F. H. Knight, trans.) (1924). New York: Collier's.

————(1968) Economy and Society (3 vols.) (G. Roth and C. Wittich, eds.; G. Roth et al., trans.) (1922). New York: Bedminster.

Weitman, S. R. (1966) "The sociological thesis of Tocqueville's 'The Old Regime and the Revolution.'" Social Research 33: 389-406.

White, H. (1973) Metahistory: The Historical Imagination in Nineteenth-Century Europe. Baltimore: Johns Hopkins University Press.

White, L. D. (1954) The Jacksonians: A Study in Administrative History 1829-1861. New York: Macmillan.

Whyte, W. H, Jr. (1956) The Organization Man. New York: Simon & Schuster.

Wilson, J. (1983) Social Theory. Englewood Cliffs, NJ: Prentice-Hall.

Winthrop, D. (1981) "Tocqueville's 'Old Regime': political history." Review of Politics 43: 88-111.

Winton, C. A. (1974) Theory and Measurement in Sociology. New York: John Wiley.

Wolin, S. S. (1960) Politics and Vision: Continuity and Innovation in Western Political Thought. Boston: Little, Brown.

Wood, G. S. (1969) The Creation of the American Republic 1776-1787. Chapel Hill: University of North Carolina Press.

Zeitlin, I. M. (1971) Liberty, Equality, and Revolution in Alexis de Tocqueville. Boston: Little, Brown.

Name Index

Almond, Gabriel, 13
America: See the United States of America
Amerindians: See also Indians, 36-37, 47, 59, 127
Aron, Raymond, 16, 22-24
Avineri, Shlomo, 99

Baker, Russell, 13
Bell, Daniel C., 16
Bellah, Robert N., 124
Bendix, Reinhard, 14, 16-17, 24, 129
Birmingham, England, 89
Boorstin, Daniel J., 13
Bryce, James, 17-19
Burke, Edmund, 39-40

Canada, 33, 71; and the United States compared, 42
Christianity, 44, 72-74, 94, 120-121; and egoism, 74; and morality, 72-74
Collins, Randall R., 12, 15-16, 19, 23-24, 102, 124, 129, 135, 139
Collins, Randall and Michael Makowsky, 12, 16
Commager, Henry Steele, 18

Dahl, Robert A., 14, 101
Dahrendorf, Ralf, 16
Davies, James C., 15
Democracy in America (Democracy), 62, 78-79, 84, 93, 128, 109; purpose of, 29; Volumes 1 and 2 compared, 51
Dilthey, Wilhelm, 12
The Division of Labor in Society, 113-114, 117-120
Drescher, Seymour, 25, 100
Durkheim, Emile, 15, 20-25; abnormal division of labor, 111, 114, 105-106, 126; anomie, 114-115; beliefs (religious), 122-123; biological reductionism, rejection of, 109; conflict, 111; despotism (tyranny), 118, 125; dualism of human nature, 111; education, 127; egoism, 115, 126; evolutionary structural-functionalism, 103; evolutionism, 103, 105, 107, 121; forces, 128; freedom, 112; French Revolution, 120; functionalism, 107-108, 111, 120-122, 124, 128; idealist conception of society, 103-104, 108, 121; individual and society (the social) as opposing forces, 110-111, 113, 116-117; individuality, 114, 116-118, 120, 126;

interaction, 103, 109, 112-114, 122; mechanical and organic solidarity, 112-114, 117; mechanical solidarity, 113, 121; modern society, 123, 126-127; morality (moral rules), 113, 123, 126; normal versus abnormal (pathological), 105-106, 111; organic society, 117, 119, 125-127; organic solidarity, 117, 119, 126-127; primitive and modern society compared, 112, 114, 116, 126; primitive society, 121, 123, 126-127; reification in, 108; rites (religious), 122-123, 126; ritual solidarity, 124; science, 116, 120, 124-125; science of ethics, 124-125; secondary groups (voluntary associations), 114, 117-119; social force and forces, 104, 110-113, 116, 118, 120, 123, 126; social psychology, 110, 115; social power, 110-112, 116; solidarity, 112-113, 122; state, 111, 118-119; substratum and superstructure, 103; symbols, 120, 122-123; Tocqueville (cited by Durkheim), 119

Eberts, Paul R. and Robert A. Witton, 18, 23
The Elementary Forms of the Religious Life (The Elementary Forms), 120, 122
England: and France and America compared, 83, 111; and France compared, 39, 41, 79, 81, 83, 106; and the United States compared, 39-40; English and French radicals compared, 94; industrialization in, 88-89

France, 29; and the United States compared, 51, 78, 88, 125
French Revolution, 33, 42-43, 45, 48-49, 52, 58, 79, 81, 87-88, 90, 92, 96-97, 110, 120, 129, 141, 144

Gargan, Edward T., 12, 25, 101
Germany, 35, 81
Gibbs, Jack P., 20-21
Gobineau, Arthur, 29-30, 36-38, 47, 58
Goldstein, Doris S., 78
Great (European) Revolution, 34

Hartz, Louis, 13
Herr, Robert, 78
Hinduism, 121-122
Horowitz, Irving Louis, 14, 128
Huntington, Samuel P., 14, 41

155

Subject Index

About the Author

WHITNEY POPE was an early entrant to the University of Chicago. After receiving three degrees (a high school graduation certificate, two college degrees, and an MA) from Chicago, Professor Pope took his Ph.D. at the University of California, Berkeley. Currently, he is a member of the Sociology Department at Indiana University. He has had a number of research grants, served as Associate Editor of *The American Sociological Review*, and published articles in the discipline's leading journals. His first book, *Durkheim's "Suicide": A Classic Analyzed,* was published in 1976 by the University of Chicago Press. His current research interests include theory, suicide, and political economy.

Professor Pope resides in Bloomington, Indiana, with his wife, who is a former Director of Women's Studies at Indiana University and is currently a member of the Afro-American Department. He and his wife have four children: the oldest daughter, Lucetta, is now in law school; the two middle children, a second daughter, Delanie, and the oldest son, Whitney, are both in college, and the youngest son, Braxton, is still at home.